The
Pyramid
Principle

FT Prentice Hall

FINANCIAL TIMES

In an increasingly competitive world, we believe it's quality of thinking that gives you the edge – an idea that opens new doors, a technique that solves a problem, or an insight that simply makes sense of it all. The more you know, the smarter and faster you can go.

That's why we work with the best minds in business and finance to bring cutting-edge thinking and best learning practice to a global market.

Under a range of leading imprints, including *Financial Times Prentice Hall*, we create world-class print publications and electronic products bringing our readers knowledge, skills and understanding, which can be applied whether studying or at work.

To find out more about Pearson Education publications, or tell us about the books you'd like to find, you can visit us at **www.pearsoned.co.uk**

PEARSON

Education

Barbara Minto

The

Pyramid

Principle

LOGIC IN WRITING AND THINKING

FT Prentice Hall
FINANCIAL TIMES

An imprint of Pearson Education

Harlow, England • London • New York • Boston • San Francisco • Toronto • Sydney • Singapore • Hong Kong
Tokyo • Seoul • Taipei • New Delhi • Cape Town • Madrid • Mexico City • Amsterdam • Munich • Milan

Pearson Education Limited
Edinburgh Gate
Harlow, Essex CM20 2JE
Tel: +44 (0)1279 623623
Fax: +44 (0)1279 431059

Website: www.pearsoned.co.uk

First published in the USA by Minto International Inc. 1987
First published in the UK in 1991
Second edition published 1995
Third edition published 2002
This revised edition published 2009

ISBN: 978-0-273-71051-6

British Library Cataloguing in Publication Data
A CIP catalogue record for this book is available from the British Library

10 9 8 7 6 5 4 3
12 11 10 09

Typeset by Pantek Arts Ltd, Maidstone, Kent.
Printed and bound in Great Britain by Henry Ling Limited, at the Dorset Press, Dorchester, DT1 1HD

The publishers' policy is to use paper manufactured from sustainable forests.

'There is

nothing so useful

as a **good theory**.'

KURT LEWIN

Contents

About the author

Barbara Minto grew up in Cleveland, Ohio. She began her career on the staff of Cyrus Eaton, the industrialist who founded the famous Pugwash Conferences of nuclear scientists. Working as part of the team that organized and ran the conferences, she received sound training in tackling the problems of communicating clearly on technical subjects.

In 1961 she left Mr. Eaton to attend the Harvard Business School, returning to Cleveland in 1963 to join McKinsey & Company, the international management consulting firm, as their first female consultant. Her ability to write was noted, and she was transferred to London in 1966, to concentrate on developing the writing skills of their growing European staff. All reports at that time were written in English, and it was thought that consultants not writing in their first language would experience special difficulties.

However, it became apparent to her very quickly that the writing difficulties in Düsseldorf and Paris were the same as those in New York and Cleveland. The problem was not so much to get the language right as to get the thinking clear. This insight led her to concentrate on discovering the structures of thinking that must underlie clear writing, and eventually to develop the ideas that make up this book.

She still lives in London, but has since 1973 run her own firm, Minto International, Inc. She specializes in teaching The Pyramid Principle to people whose major training is in business or the professions, but whose jobs nevertheless require them to produce complex reports, analyses, memorandums, or presentations.

She has taught her course to most of the major consulting firms in the United States and Europe, as well as to many of the country's largest corporations. She has also lectured at the Harvard, Stanford, Chicago, and London business schools, and at the State University of New York.

Preface

This book proposes to tell you how to use The Pyramid Principle to write a clear business document. Writing anything clearly consists of two steps: first, decide the point you want to make, then put it into words. So long as you know the point, you rarely have a problem stating it:

- Please leave two quarts today.
- I'll meet you at 12:30 at Mario's.
- Call your wife.

But you can run into trouble when you have to sort through a series of points to come to an overall conclusion:

> John Collins telephoned to say that he can't make the meeting at 3:00. Hal Johnson says he doesn't mind making it later, or even tomorrow, but not before 10:30, and Don Clifford's secretary says that Clifford won't return from Frankfurt until tomorrow, late. The Conference Room is booked tomorrow, but free Thursday. Thursday at 11:00 looks to be a good time. Is that OK for you?

What the author has done here is what most people do when they write. He has used the writing process as a device to formulate his thinking. As a device it works quite well, in fact, but the result is a bit hard on the reader, who is forced to plow through several irrelevant sentences before he finds the point. How much easier if the note had read:

> Could we reschedule today's meeting to Thursday at 11:00? This would be more convenient for Collins and Johnson, and would also permit Clifford to be present.

Alas, to get from the first example to the second means double work for both the author and his secretary, and most people feel it is not really worth the effort for such a short note. No doubt they're right. But what happens when, instead of the document's being one paragraph long, it is two or three pages? Usually the author feels it would take too long to revise it, and in any case he's often not sure just how to go about doing the revision. Much easier, he decides, to leave it to the reader to sort through the points and pull out the message for himself.

Until recently few readers actually complained about this attitude on the part of their correspondents. Most took it for granted that this was how business writing was supposed to look, since it resembled what they themselves had learned to produce by careful copying of their superiors. Indeed, I can recall once telling a consultant that his 2-hour presentation on a company's new organization structure was boring. He replied:

> 'What you don't realize is that people come expecting it to be boring. They're used to it.'

Perhaps. But the time wasted is enormous, and continual exposure to badly written, boring documents can only be soul destroying. As one commentator sympathetically noted, 'The myth that businessmen don't read is nonsense. They read a lot. But what they read is illiterate.'

For the average business or professional writer, producing more literate memos and reports does not mean writing shorter sentences or choosing better words. Rather, it means formally separating the thinking process from the writing process, so that you can complete your thinking *before* you begin to write. And that's what this book will tell you how to do.

Essentially it will tell you that it is the order in which you present your thinking that makes your writing clear or unclear, and that you cause confusion in the reader's mind when you do not impose the proper order. Imposing the proper order means creating a comprehensive structure that identifies the major ideas and their flow, and organizes the minor ideas to support them.

The key skill, then, is to be able to recognize which are your major and which your minor ideas, and to work out their relationships within the structure. The demands of logic and the limitations of a reader's ability to take in information dictate that this structure will always be pyramidal in shape – hence The Pyramid Principle.

Part One will both explain this principle and show you how to use it to build a beginning pyramid. Part Two will show you how to use your knowledge of the pyramid rules to look critically at this structure, find its logical flaws, and push your thinking creatively so that you end up saying precisely what you mean.

The approach is applicable to any document in which your purpose is to get your thinking across clearly. Applying it, however, requires considerable discipline. Nevertheless, by deliberately forcing yourself to think first and write later in the manner it suggests, you should be able quite dramatically (a) to cut down the time you normally need to produce a final draft, (b) to increase its clarity, and (c) to decrease its length.

The

Pyramid

Principle

I	Logic in Writing

Introduction

to part I

One of the least pleasant aspects of a professional person's job is the need to put things in writing. Almost everyone finds it a chore and wishes he were better at it. And many people are told specifically that they need to improve if they want to progress.

The reason most people don't improve is that they assume that writing more clearly means writing simpler, more direct sentences. And it is true that the sentences in their documents are often overlong and unwieldy. Moreover, their language is frequently too technical or too abstract, and their paragraphs on occasion are awkwardly developed.

But these are weaknesses of style, and it is notoriously difficult for a person who has completed the formal part of his education to change his writing style. Not that it cannot be done; rather, it's like learning to type. It requires a good many repetitive exercises, for which most on-the-job writers in industry and government simply cannot find the time. As a result, they continue to be told they need to write 'more clearly.'

However, there is a second cause of unclear writing, far more pervasive than the first, and much easier to correct. This relates to the structure of the document – the order in which the sentences appear regardless of whether they are well or poorly written. If a person's writing is unclear, it is most likely because the ordering of the ideas conflicts with the capability of the reader's mind to process them.

This capability is the same for everyone, whether reader or writer, so that learning to accommodate it is a relatively easy task. And invariably, the writer who forces himself to match the structure of his writing to that of his reader's mind also finds that he has clarified his own thinking sufficiently to write less awkward sentences.

This first section of the book explains why the structure in a reader's mind will always be a pyramid, and what the logical substructures are that make up that pyramid. It tells you how to use this knowledge to identify the ideas you need to include in a particular document, and to structure a clear relationship between them. Finally, it tells you how to highlight your structure so that the ideas and their relationships will be easy to see at a glance.

Why a pyramid structure?

The person who seeks to learn what you think about a particular subject by reading what you have to say about it faces a complex task. Even if your document is a short one – say only about 2 single-spaced pages – it will contain roughly 100 sentences. He must take in each of these, digest them, relate them, and hold them together. He will invariably find the job easier if they come to him as a pyramid, beginning at the top and working downward. This conclusion reflects some fundamental findings about the way the mind works. Specifically:

- The mind automatically sorts information into distinctive pyramidal groupings in order to comprehend it.
- Any grouping of ideas is easier to comprehend if it arrives presorted into its pyramid.
- This suggests that every written document should be deliberately structured to form a pyramid of ideas.

The sections following explain what I mean by a pyramid of ideas.

Sorting into pyramids

That the mind automatically imposes order on everything around it has long been recognized. Essentially, it tends to see any sequence of things that occur together as belonging together, and therefore sets about imposing a logical pattern on them. The Greeks, for example, demonstrated the tendency by looking up at the stars and seeing outlines of figures instead of pinpoints of light.

The mind will group together any series of items that it sees as having a 'common fate' – because they share similar characteristics or are near the same place. Take these six dots for example:

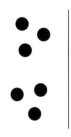

When looking casually at them, everyone sees two groups of three dots each, primarily because some of the distances between the dots are smaller than others.

The value of seeing things in logical units is, of course, immense. To demonstrate, read the following pairs of nouns,* which are normally not related to each other.

LAKE	• SUGAR
BOOT	• PLATE
GIRL	• KANGAROO
PENCIL	• GASOLINE
PALACE	• BICYCLE
RAILROAD	• ELEPHANT
BOOK	• TOOTHPASTE

Now try to 'organize' them by picturing a situation in which each one might be associated – such as the sugar being dissolved in the lake or the boot sitting on the plate. Then cover up the list on the right-hand side and try to remember them through reading the list on the left-hand side. Most people find that they can recall them all without hesitation.

The same organizing phenomenon takes place when you are either listening to or reading ideas. You assume the ideas that appear together, one after the other, belong together, and attempt to impose a logical pattern on them. The pattern will always be that of a pyramid because this is the only form that meets your mind's need to

- Stop at the magical number seven.
- State the logic of the relationship.

---

* Based on a series given in *Gestalt Psychology* by Wolfgang Kohler (Liveright Publishing: New York) 1970.

The Magical Number Seven

There is a limit to the number of ideas you can comprehend at any one time. For example, think of deciding to leave your warm, comfortable living room to buy this week's racing form. 'I think I'll go pick up a magazine,' you say to your wife, 'Is there anything you want while I'm out?'

'Gosh. I have such a taste for grapes after all those ads on television,' she says as you walk toward the closet to get your coat, 'and maybe you ought to get some more milk.' You take your coat from the closet as she walks into the kitchen.

'Let me look in the cupboard to see if we have enough potatoes and, oh yes, I know we're out of eggs. Let me see, yes, we do need potatoes.' You put on your coat and walk toward the door.

'Carrots,' she calls out, 'and maybe some oranges.' You open the door. 'Butter.' You walk down the stairs. 'Apples.' You get into the car. 'And sour cream.' 'Is that all?' 'Yes, dear, thank you.'

Now, without reading the passage over, can you remember any of the nine items your wife asked you to buy? Most men come back with the racing form and the grapes.

The major problem is that you've run into the magic number seven. This is a phrase coined by George A. Miller in his treatise, 'The Magical Number Seven, Plus or Minus Two.'* What he points out is that the mind cannot hold more than about seven items in its short-term memory at any one time. Some minds can hold as many as nine items, while others can hold only five (I'm a five myself). A convenient number is three, but of course the easiest number is one.

What this means is that when the mind sees the number of items with which it is being presented begin to rise above four or five, it starts to group them into logical categories so that they can be retained. In this case, it would probably put the items into categories that reflect the sections of the supermarket you would need to visit.

To demonstrate how this helps, read the list below and categorize each idea in this way as you come to it. You will very likely find that you remember them all.

* Miller, George A. *The Psychology of Communication: Seven Essays* (Basic Books: Pa.) 1967.

GRAPES   ORANGES
MILK   BUTTER
POTATOES   APPLES
EGGS   SOUR CREAM
CARROTS

If you try to visualize this process, you will see that you have created a set of pyramids of logically related items.

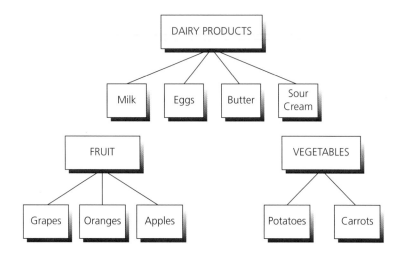

The need to state the logic

Now clearly, it is not enough simply to group the ideas in a logical way without also stating to yourself what the logic of the relationship is. The point in grouping was not just to move from a set of nine items to separate sets of four, two, and three items. That still comes to nine. What you want to do is move above the nine, to three.

This means that instead of remembering each of the nine items, you remember only the three categories into which they fall. You are thinking one level of abstraction higher, but because the thought is at a higher level, it suggests the items below it. And, because the relationship is not a contrived one as was the case in the exercise about the lake and the sugar, it is much easier to keep in mind.

All mental processes (e.g., thinking, remembering, problem solving) apparently utilize this grouping and summarizing process, so that the information in a person's mind might be thought of as being organized into one giant conglomeration of related pyramids. If you think about communicating to that mind, you can see that the problem is one of ensuring that what you say will fit somewhere into the existing pyramids.

Now we come to the real problem of communicating. You can 'see' these groupings of items quite clearly. To communicate them means to ensure that the other person 'sees' them in the same way. But, as was the case with your wife, you can only present them one by one. Surely, the most efficient way to do this would be to present the category first and then the items. That is, to order the ideas from the top down.

Ordering from the top down

Controlling the sequence in which you present your ideas is the single most important act necessary to clear writing. The clearest sequence is always to give the summarizing idea before you give the individual ideas being summarized. I cannot emphasize this point too much.

Remember that the reader (or listener) can only take the sentences in one at a time. You know he will assume that those ideas that appear together logically belong together. If you do not tell him in advance what the relationship is, but simply give the ideas one at a time, he will automatically look for similarities by which he can group the points being expressed, so that he can explain to himself the significance of the groupings.

Alas, people being as diverse in background and understanding as they are, they rarely put exactly the same interpretation on your groupings as you do. Indeed, they not infrequently find that they can't see any relationship at all between the ideas in a set. Even if they think exactly as you do, you are making their reading more difficult, since they must supply what is unstated.

Let me demonstrate how confusing any order other than top down is with an example. Suppose I join you to have a beer in the pub, and apropos of nothing in particular, say:

> I was in Zurich last week – you know what a conservative city Zurich is – and we went out to lunch at an outdoor restaurant. Do you know that within 15 minutes I must have seen 15 people with either a beard or a moustache.

Now, I have given you a piece of information, and without realizing it you will automatically make some assumptions about the reason for my giving you that information. In other words, you will see this statement as part of a group of ideas not yet expressed, and prepare your mind to receive the rest by assuming a probable purpose behind the statement. This expectancy reduces the strain of analyzing each succeeding idea for all its attributes; you look only for the one in common with what has gone before.

Thus, you might think such things as, 'She's talking about how uncon-servative Zurich is getting,' or 'She's going to compare Zurich with other cities,' or even, 'She's hung up on beards and moustaches.' Regardless of what reaction you have, the point is that your mind is waiting for further information on one of those same subjects, whatever it turns out to be. Seeing that blank look on your face, I then go on to say:

> And you know, if you walk around any New York office you can rarely find even one person who doesn't have sideburns or a moustache.

Now what am I getting at? I seem to be comparing not cities as such, but cities in which we have offices; and instead of just beards and moustaches I seem to be including all manner of facial hair. 'Probably,' you're thinking, 'she disapproves of the new style. Or maybe she's going to compare the styles in various offices. Or maybe she's surprised at the amount tolerated in the consulting profession.' In any case, you mutter something noncom-mittal in reply, and thus encouraged I go on to state:

> And of course facial hair has been a part of the London scene for at least 10 years.

'Ah,' you think, 'at last I see what she's getting at. She's trying to make the point that London is ahead of all the other cities,' and you tell me so. Perfectly logical, but it's wrong; that's not what I was getting at at all. In fact, what I was getting at was this:

> You know it's incredible to me the degree to which facial hair has become such an accepted part of business life.
> In Zurich . . .
> In New York . . .
> And of course in London . . .

See how much more easily you can comprehend the group of ideas in the way I mean you to once the framework within which to judge the rela-tionship between them has been given to you? In a manner outside anyone's control, the reader is going to look for a structure connecting the ideas as they come to him. To make sure he finds the one you intended, you must tell him in advance what it is – to make sure he knows what to look for. Otherwise he is likely either to see an unintended relationship, or worse, none at all, in which case you have both wasted your time.

As an example of this latter situation, look at the main points of the opening paragraphs of an article on equal pay for women:

> Granted equal pay, women could finish off worse than before – i.e., there could be a wider rather than narrower gap between average earnings of women and men than today.
> - Equal pay means equal pay for the same job or equal pay for equal value of work (to the employer).
> - Applying either interpretation means either:
>   Compelling employers to act in their own self-interest, or
>   Ending restrictive practices by male workers.

Here you are given five ideas between which the connecting relationship is unclear, despite the fact that the author has 'started at the top,' as he sees it. Can you not feel your mind scrabbling about trying to find a relationship, coming to the conclusion that there is none, and giving up in disgust? The mental strain is simply too great.

You must recognize that a reader, no matter how intelligent he is, has only a limited amount of mental energy available to him. Some of it will be used up just recognizing and interpreting the words, a further amount seeing the relationships between the ideas, and whatever is left comprehending their significance.

You can economize his need to spend time on the first two activities by presenting the ideas so that they can be comprehended with the least possible mental effort. To sequence them instead so that the mind has to go backward and forward to make connections is simply bad manners, and most readers react by refusing to do so.

To summarize, a reader remembers from the top down as a matter of course. He also comprehends more readily if ideas are presented from the top down. All of this suggests that the clearest written documents will be those that consistently present their information from the top down, in a pyramidal structure.

Thinking from the bottom up

If you are going to group and summarize all your information and present it in a top-down manner, it would seem your document would have to look something like the structure in Exhibit 1. The boxes stand for the individual ideas you want to present, with your thinking having begun at the lowest level by forming sentences that you grouped logically into paragraphs. You then grouped the paragraphs into sections, and the sections into the total memorandum represented by a single thought at the top.

If you think for a moment about what you actually do when you write, you can see that you develop your major ideas by thinking in this bottom-up manner. At the very lowest level in the pyramid, you group together your sentences, each containing an individual idea, into paragraphs. Let us suppose you bring together six sentences into one paragraph. The reason you bring together those six sentences and no others will clearly be that you see a logical relationship between them. And that logical relationship will always be that they are all needed to express the single idea of the paragraph, which is effectively a summary of them. You would not, for example, bring together five sentences on finance and one on tennis, because their relevance to each other would be difficult to express in a single summary sentence.

Stating this summary sentence moves you up one level of abstraction and allows you to think of the paragraph as containing one point rather than six. With this act of efficiency you now group together, say, three paragraphs, each containing a single thought at a level of abstraction one step higher than that of the individual sentences. The reason you form a section out of these three paragraphs and no others is that you see a logical relationship between them. And the relationship is once again that they are all needed to express the single idea of the section, which again will be a summary of the three ideas in the paragraphs below them.

Exactly the same thinking holds true in bringing the sections together to form the document. You have three sections grouped together (each of which has been built up from groups of paragraphs, which in turn have been built up from groups of sentences) because they are all needed to express the single idea of the memorandum, which in turn is a summary of them.

Since you will continue grouping and summarizing until you have no more relationships to make, it is clear that every document you write will always be structured to support only one single thought – the one that summarizes your final set of groupings. This should be the major point you want to make, and all the ideas grouped underneath – provided you have built the structure properly – will serve to explain or defend that point in ever greater detail.

Fortunately, you can define in advance whether or not you have built the structure properly by checking to see whether your ideas relate to each other in a way that would permit them to form pyramidal groups. Specifically, they must obey three rules:

Exhibit 1 Ideas in writing should always form a pyramid under a single thought

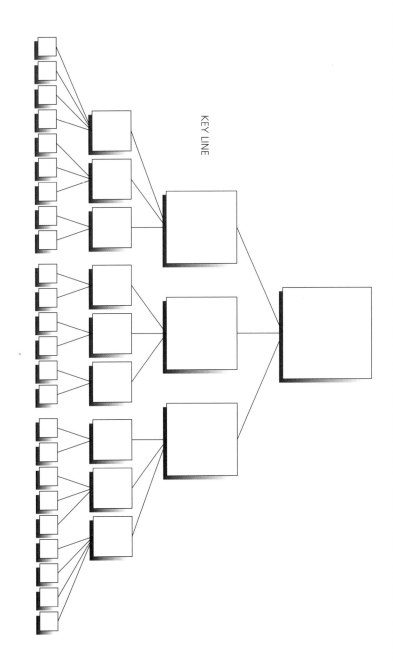

KEY LINE

1 Ideas at any level in the pyramid must always be summaries of the ideas grouped below them.

2 Ideas in each grouping must always be the same kind of idea.

3 Ideas in each grouping must always be logically ordered.

Let me explain why these rules 'must always' apply:

1 *Ideas at any level in the pyramid must always be summaries of the ideas grouped below them.* The first rule reflects the fact that the major activity you carry out in thinking and writing is that of abstracting to create a new idea out of the ideas grouped below. As we saw above, the point of a paragraph is a summary of its sentences, just as the point of a section is a summary of the points of its paragraphs, etc. However, if you are going to be able to draw a point out of the grouped sentences or paragraphs, these groupings must have been properly formed in the first place. That's where rules 2 and 3 come in.

2 *Ideas in each grouping must always be the same kind of idea.* If what you want to do is raise your thinking only one level of abstraction above a grouping of ideas, then the ideas in the grouping must be logically the same. For example, you can logically categorize apples and pears one level up as fruits; you can similarly think of tables and chairs as furniture. But what if you wanted to group together apples and chairs? You cannot do so at the very next level of abstraction, since that is already taken by fruit and furniture. Thus, you would have to move to a much higher level and call them 'things' or 'inanimate objects,' either of which is far too broad to indicate the logic of the grouping.

In writing you want to state the idea directly implied by the logic of the grouping, so the ideas in the grouping must all fall into the same logical category. Thus, if the first idea in a grouping is a reason for doing something, the other ideas in the same grouping must also be reasons for doing the same thing. If the first idea is a step in a process, the rest of the ideas in the grouping must also be steps in the same process. If the first idea is a problem in the company, the others in the grouping must be related problems, and so on.

A shortcut in checking your groupings is to be sure that you can clearly label the ideas with a plural noun. Thus, you will find that all the ideas in the grouping will turn out to be things like recommendations, or reasons, or problems, or changes to be made. There is no limitation on the kinds of ideas that may be grouped, but the ideas in each grouping must be of the same kind, able to be described by one plural noun. How you make sure you get like kinds of ideas grouped together each time is explained more fully in Part Two, Chapters 7, 8, and 9.

3 Ideas in each grouping must always be logically ordered. That is, there must be a specific reason why the second idea comes second, and cannot come first or third. How you determine proper order is explained in detail in Chapter 7, *Questioning the Order of the Ideas*. Essentially it says that there are only four possible logical ways in which to order a set of ideas:

- Deductively (major premise, minor premise, conclusion).
- Chronologically (first, second, third).
- Structurally (Boston, New York, Washington).
- Comparatively (first most important, second most important, etc.).

The order you choose reflects the analytical process you used to form the grouping. If it was formed by reasoning deductively, the ideas go in argument order; if by working out cause-and-effect relationships, in time order; if by commenting on an existing structure, the order dictated by the structure; and if by categorizing, order of importance. Since these four activities – reasoning deductively, working out cause-and-effect relationships, dividing a whole into its parts, and categorizing – are the only analytical activities the mind can perform, these are the only orders it can impose.

Essentially, then, the key to clear writing is to slot your ideas into this pyramidal form and test them against the rules before you begin to write. If any of the rules is broken, it is an indication that there is a flaw in your thinking, or that the ideas have not been fully developed, or that they are not related in a way that will make their message instantly clear to the reader. You can then work on refining them until they do obey the rules, thus eliminating the need for vast amounts of rewriting later on.

The substructures within the pyramid

As Chapter 1 explained, a clear piece of writing establishes a rigid set of relationships between its ideas, so that they will form a comprehensive pyramidal structure (see Exhibit 1). It then presents the ideas to the reader, starting at the top and working down each leg.

Because of the specificity of the pyramid rules, if you know what your ideas are before you begin to write, you can relatively easily form them into a proper pyramid. Most people when they sit down to write, however, have only a hazy notion of their ideas (if that). Nor should they expect much more. No one can know precisely what he thinks until he has been forced to symbolize it – either by saying it out loud or by writing it down – and even then the first statement of the idea is likely to be less precise than he can eventually make it.

Consequently, you cannot hope just to sit down and start arranging your ideas into a pyramid. You have to discover them first. But the pyramid dictates a rigid set of substructures that can serve to speed the discovery process. These are:

- The vertical relationship between points and subpoints.
- The horizontal relationship within a set of subpoints.
- The narrative flow of the introduction.

Let me explain the exact nature of these relationships and then, in Chapter 3, tell you how to use them to discover, sort, and arrange your ideas so that they will be clear, first to yourself and then to your reader.

The vertical relationship

Some of the most obvious facts in the world take years to work their way into people's minds. A good example is what happens when you read. Normal prose is written one-dimensionally, in that it presents one sentence after another, more or less vertically down the page. But that vertical follow-on obscures the fact that the ideas occur at various levels of abstraction. Any idea below the main point will always have both a vertical and a horizontal relationship to the other ideas in the document.

The vertical relationship serves marvelously to help capture the reader's attention. It permits you to set up a question/answer dialogue that will pull him with great interest through your reasoning. Why can we be so sure the reader will be interested? Because he will be forced to respond logically to your ideas.

What you put into each box in the pyramid structure is an idea. I define an idea as a statement that raises a question in the reader's mind because you are telling him something he does not know. (Since people do not generally read to find out what they already know, it is fair to state that your primary purpose in writing any document will always be to tell people what they do not know.)

Making a statement to a reader that tells him something he does not know will automatically raise a logical question in his mind – for example, Why? or How? or Why do you say that? The writer is now obliged to answer that question horizontally on the line below. In his answer, however, he will still be telling the reader things he does not know, so he will raise further questions that must again be answered on the line below.

The writer will continue to write, raising and answering questions, until he reaches a point at which he judges the reader will have no more logical questions. (The reader will not necessarily agree with the writer's reasoning when he's reached this point, but he will have followed it clearly, which is the best any writer can hope for.) The writer is now free to leave the first leg of the pyramid and go back up to the Key Line to answer the original question raised by the point in the top box.

The way to ensure total reader attention, therefore, is to refrain from raising any questions in the reader's mind before you are ready to answer them. Or from answering questions before you have raised them. For example, any time a document presents a section captioned 'Our Assumptions' before it gives the major points, you can be sure the writer is answering questions the reader could not possibly have had an opportunity to raise. Consequently, the information will have to be repeated (or reread) at the relevant point in the dialogue.

The pyramid structure almost magically forces you to present information only as the reader needs it. Let me take you through a couple of examples. Exhibit 2, the first one, is a humorous one, from an article by G. K. Chesterton. It will give you an idea of how the question/answer technique works to hold the reader's attention without burdening you with the need to think about the relevance of the content.

Exhibit 2 The pyramid structure establishes a question/answer dialogue

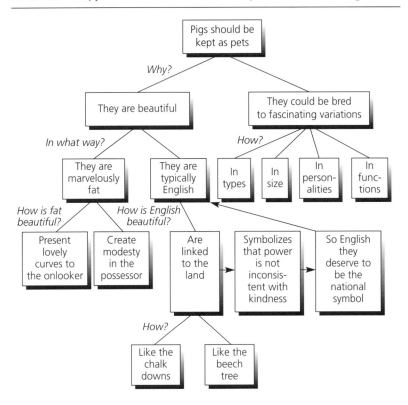

Chesterton says that pigs should be kept as pets, the reader asks Why? Chesterton says, 'For two reasons: First, they are extremely beautiful, and second, they could be bred to fascinating variations.'

Reader:	Since when are pigs beautiful?
Chesterton:	They're beautiful because they're marvelously fat and they're typically English.
Reader:	What's beautiful about being fat?
Chesterton:	It presents lovely curves to the onlooker and it creates modesty in the possessor.

Now at this point, while you clearly do not agree with Chesterton's argument, you can at least see what it is. It is clear to you why he says what he says, and there are no more questions in your mind. Consequently, he can move on to the next leg of his argument – that pigs are beautiful because they are typically English.

> *Reader:*   Why is typically English beautiful?
>
> *Chesterton:* Pigs are linked to the land; this link symbolizes that power is not inconsistent with kindness; that attitude is so English and so beautiful that they deserve to be the national symbol.

Again, you may have a certain prejudice against the sentiment, but it is clear to you why he says what he says. And it is clear because the grouping of ideas sticks to doing its job of answering the question raised by the point above. The last section, about variations, enters the mind equally clearly.

You can see this same technique at work in a piece of business writing (Exhibit 3). Here we have the structure of a 20-page memorandum recommending the purchase of an Internet Cafe franchise. It is a good buy for three reasons, and underneath each reason is the answer to the further question raised in the reader's mind by making this point. The reasoning is so clearly

Exhibit 3 All documents should reflect the question/answer dialogue

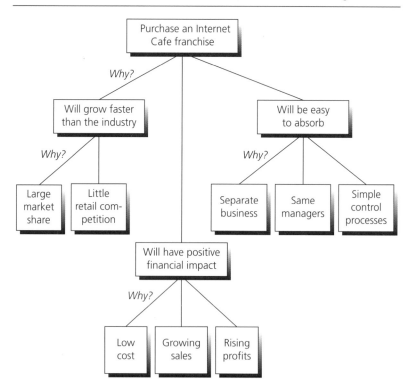

stated that the reader is in a position to determine whether he disagrees with the writer's reasoning, and to raise logical questions concerning it.

To summarize, then, a great value of the pyramid structure is that it forces visual recognition of this vertical relationship on you as you work out your thinking. Any point you make must raise a question in the reader's mind, which you must answer horizontally on the line below.

The horizontal relationship

In deciding what to say on the line below, not only must the points you include answer the question raised by the point above, they must also answer it logically. That is, they must present a clear inductive or deductive argument, one or the other, but not both at once. These are the only two types of logical relationships possible in a grouping.

A deductive grouping presents an argument in successive steps. That is, the first idea makes a statement about a situation that exists in the world today. The second idea comments on the subject or the predicate of that statement, and the third idea states the implication of those two situations existing in the world at the same time. Thus, the grouping would have the following form:

- Men are mortal.
- Socrates is a man.
- Therefore Socrates is mortal.

To move up a level of abstraction from a deductive grouping, you summarize the argument, with your summary resting heavily on the final point: 'Because Socrates is a man he is mortal.'

An inductive grouping, by contrast, will take a set of ideas that are related simply by virtue of the fact that you can describe them all by the same plural noun (reasons for, reasons against, steps, problems, etc.). The form of this argument would be:

- French tanks are at the Polish border.
- German tanks are at the Polish border.
- Russian tanks are at the Polish border.

To move upward here, you draw an inference based on your assessment of what is the same about the points – i.e., they are all warlike movements against Poland. Thus, your inference would be something like 'Poland is about to be invaded by tanks.'

In writing, if your answer is deductive you know you must have an argument in which the second point comments on the subject or predicate of the first, and the third point draws a 'therefore' from the previous two. If it is inductive, you know the ideas in the grouping must be logically alike and can be designated by a plural noun.

Given this knowledge, you can see that any one idea in the pyramid implies all the others. Consequently, you could start to build your pyramid anywhere, with a single idea, adding the other ideas as they were demanded – either up or down or sideways. But there is one more thing you need to know before you venture off to build a pyramid of your own. And that is the question to which your document must give the answer. You determine that by tracing the narrative flow of the introduction.

The introductory flow

We saw earlier that the pyramid structure permits you to carry on a question/answer dialogue with your reader. This question/answer dialogue cannot be counted on to engage his interest unless the statement that starts it off is relevant to him. The only way you can be confident of its relevance is to make sure that it directly answers a question you have identified as already existing in his mind.

I said earlier that you write primarily to tell people what they don't know. But a reader wants to find out what he doesn't know only if he needs to do so. If he has no need, he will have no question, and vice versa.

Thus, you make sure your document is of interest by directing it toward answering a question that already exists in the reader's mind, or that would exist if he thought for a minute about what is going on around him. The introduction identifies that question by tracing the history of its origin.

Since this history will be in the form of a narrative of events, it should follow the classic narrative pattern of development. That is, it should begin by establishing for the reader the time and place of a Situation. In that Situation something will have occurred (known as the Complication) that caused him to raise (or would cause him to raise) the Question to which your document will give him the Answer.

This classic pattern of story-telling – Situation, Complication, Question, Answer – permits you to make sure that you and the reader are 'standing in the same place' before you take him by the hand and lead him through your thinking. It also gives you a clear focus for the point at the top of your document, and thus a means of judging that you are conveying the right message in the most direct way.

To illustrate, here is an introduction of the kind normally seen in business:

The purpose of this memorandum is to pull together some ideas for further reflection and discussion in such questions as:

1 Composition of the Board and its optimum size.

2 A conception of the broad roles of the Board and the Executive Committee, the specific responsibilities of each, and the relationships of one to the other.

3 Making the outside Board member an effective participant.

4 Some principles dealing with the selection of Board members and their tenure.

5 Alternate ways for the company to get from where it is to where it wants to be in Board and Executive Committee operations.

Note how much more easily you comprehend its purpose and message when it is forced to fit the narrative mold:

The new organization installed in October places full authority and responsibility for running the day-to-day activities of the two divisions squarely on the shoulders of the managers of those divisions. This move frees the Board to deal entirely with the broad matters of policy and planning that are its exclusive responsibility.

However, the Board has for so long oriented itself to dealing with short-term operating problems that it is not presently in a position to focus its attention on long-range strategy development. Consequently, it must consider the changes needed to permit itself to do so. Specifically, we believe it should:

• Relinquish responsibility for day-to-day operating matters to the Executive Committee

• Broaden its composition to include outside members

• Establish policies and procedures to formalize internal operation.

In summary, the introduction tells the reader, in story form, what he already knows or could reasonably be expected to know about the subject you are discussing, and thus reminds him of the question he has to which he can expect the document to give him an answer. The story sets forth the Situation within which a Complication developed that raised the Question to which your document will now give the Answer. Once you state the Answer (the main point at the top of your pyramid), it will raise a new question in the reader's mind that you will answer on the line below.

What does the existence of these three substructures – i.e., the vertical question/answer dialogue, the horizontal deductive or inductive logic, and the narrative introductory structure – do for you in helping you discover the ideas you need to build a pyramid? Knowing the vertical relationship, you can determine the kind of ideas you need in each grouping (i.e., those that will answer the question). Knowing the horizontal relationship, you can judge that the ideas you bring together are of a like kind (i.e., proper parts of an inductive or deductive argument). And – most important – knowing the reader's question will ensure that all the ideas you do bring together are relevant (i.e., exist only because they help to answer that question).

Naturally, you want to go about applying these insights in an orderly way, and that's what Chapter 3 will tell you how to do.

How to build a pyramid structure

3

The problem you generally face as you sit down to write is that you know roughly what you want to write about, but not specifically what you want to say or how you want to say it. This sense of uncertainty is hardly enhanced by knowing that the ideas you eventually put down, whatever they be, must end up forming a pyramid.

Nevertheless, there is a good deal that you *do* know about your end product that you can build on. To begin with, you know that you will have a sentence at the top of the pyramid that will have a subject and a predicate. You also know that the subject of that sentence will be the subject of your document.

In addition, you know that the sentence will serve as the answer to a question that already exists in the reader's mind. And that question will have arisen because of a situation (with which the reader is familiar) within which a complication developed (with which he is also familiar) that raised the question that caused you to need to write in the first place. You may even know roughly some of the points you want to make.

That is quite a bit to know. You can use this knowledge in building your pyramid either by starting at the top and working down, or by starting at the bottom and working up. The first way is generally easier than the second, and so should be tried first.

The top-down approach

It is generally easier to start at the top and work down because you begin by thinking about the things that it is easiest for you to be sure of – your subject and the reader's knowledge of it, which you will remind him of in the introduction.

You don't want simply to sit down and begin writing the opening paragraph of the introduction, however. Instead, you want to use the structure of the introductory flow to pull the right points out of your head, one at a time. To do so, I suggest you follow the procedure shown in Exhibit 4 and described below.

Exhibit 4 The elements of the structure check each other

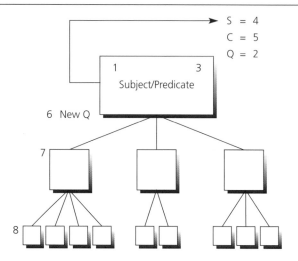

Fill in the top box
1. What Subject are you discussing?
2. What Question are you answering in
   the reader's mind about the Subject?
3. What is the Answer?

Match the Answer to the introduction
4. What is the Situation?
5. What is the Complication?
2. Do the Question and Answer still follow?

Find the key line
6. What New Question is raised by the Answer?
7. Will you answer it deductively or inductively?
7. If inductively, what is your plural noun?

Structure the support points
8. Repeat the question/answer process at this level.

1 *Draw a box*. This represents the box at the top of your pyramid.
Write down in it the subject you are discussing.

2 *Decide the Question*. Visualize your reader. To whom are you
writing, and what question do you want to have answered in his
mind about the Subject when you have finished writing?

3 *Write down the Answer*, if you know it.

4 *Identify the Situation*. Next you want to prove that you have the
clearest statement of the Question and the Answer that you can
formulate at this stage. To do that, you take the Subject, move up
to the Situation, and make the first noncontroversial statement

about it you can make. What is the first thing you can say about it to the reader that you know he will agree is true – either because he knows it, or because it is historically true and easily checkable?

5 *Develop the Complication*. Now you say to yourself, 'So What?' This should lead you to think of what happened in that Situation to raise the Question. Something went wrong, perhaps, some problem arose, or some logical discrepancy became apparent. What happened in the situation to trigger the question?

6 *Recheck the Question and Answer*. The statement of the Complication should immediately raise the Question you have already written down. If it does not, then change it to the one it does raise. Or perhaps you have the wrong Complication, or the wrong Question, and must think again.

The purpose of the entire exercise is to make sure you know what Question it is you are trying to answer. Once you have the Question, every-thing else falls into place relatively easily.

Let me demonstrate how your thinking would develop by using the tech-nique to rewrite the memorandum shown in Exhibit 5. It comes from the Accounting Department of a large beverage company in the United States.

When the company's drivers deliver the product to a customer, they send back to the Accounting Department a delivery ticket with a set of code numbers, the date, and the amount of the delivery. These delivery tickets are the basis of the billing system, which works something like this:

FIVE WEEKS			
Process ➡ delivery tickets	Send ➡ bill	Receive ➡ check	Process Payment

One of the company's customers, a hamburger emporium we'll call Big Chief, gets an awful lot of deliveries. For its own accounting purposes, it would like to keep daily track of how the bill is mounting up. It wants to know if it can't keep the delivery tickets along with each delivery, record them on a computer tape, calculate the total, and then send the tape and its check once a month to the headquarters office of the beverage com-pany. In other words, it is proposing a system that would work like this:

ONE DAY	
Receive tape ➡ and check	Process Payment

Exhibit 5 Original Big Chief Memorandum

To: Mr Robert Salmon
From: John J. Jackson
Subject: Big Chief Date: March 7, 2001

We have been requested to review the feasibility of processing Big Chief's (Parent Number 8306) N/A Delivery Tickets via tape into our National Accounts System. This processing is to be accomplished by Big Chief and us on a prepayment basis. We have completed our review of this request and our findings are as follows:

1. Our primary requirement for accepting any National Accounts data from an outside source is that we receive records in a prescribed format:

   a. Parent Number
   b. Outlet Number
   c. Ticket Number
   d. Dollar amount of each ticket
   e. Delivary Date of each ticket

   If the Parent and Outlet Numbers are not available from Big Chief, we will supply this information to them from our Customer Master File list. This information could then be incorporated into the Big Chief system for future ease in the processing of ticket data.

2. Big Chief will produce an extract program that will be run against their file (A/P Liability) to extract all ticket information presently on that file. The output file created by this program will be in a format acceptable to the N/A subsystem APNND, Cash Receipt Advice (see Record Layout). This data, in the form of a tape, will then be sent to us for balancing purposes and at the same time, Big Chief's check, accompanied by a detailed listing of the information on the tape (see Report Layout #1) will be sent to the National Accounts lock box.

   The tape received by our Data Processing Department will be balanced according to our prescribed procedures. The final result of this balancing is that t he dollar amount of the submitted check and the detail of the tape must 'zero balance' (.00).

3. Upon completion, the balanced cash tape will be processed through the National Accounts System. This will produce a matchup by ticket number against the N/A Updated Statement History file and the production of National Syrup Account Billing Statements.

The head of the Accounting Department has been asked if the change would be feasible, and has answered in his present memorandum by saying essentially, 'Here's how the new system would work,' without actually answering the question. Had you been he, and used the technique in Exhibit 4, here's what would have happened:

1 You would have drawn a box and said to yourself, 'What Subject am I discussing?' (BC request for change, Exhibit 6.)

2 What *Question* am I answering in the reader's mind about the Subject?' (Is it a good idea?)

3 What's the *Answer*? (Yes.)

4 Now let me check that that is really the Question and really the Answer by thinking through the introduction. To do that I take the Subject and move up to the *Situation*. The first sentence of the Situation must be a statement about the Subject. What is the first noncontroversial thing I can think of to say about the Subject – something I know the reader will not question, but will accept as fact? (They have requested a change in the procedure.) When you go to write the introduction out, you will of course in this paragraph explain the nature of the change, but for the purposes of working out your thinking you need only get clear the essence of the point of the paragraph.

5 Now I look at the Situation and say about it, 'So what?' This should lead me directly to a statement of the *Complication*. (You've asked me whether it makes sense.)

Exhibit 6 New Big Chief Structure 5

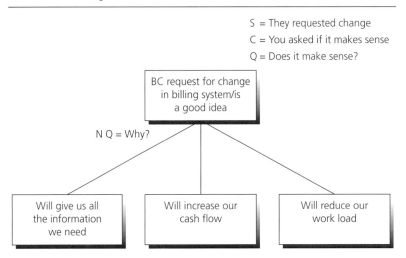

S = They requested change
C = You asked if it makes sense
Q = Does it make sense?

BC request for change in billing system/is a good idea

N Q = Why?

Will give us all the information we need

Will increase our cash flow

Will reduce our work load

The Question, (2), as you've stated it should now be the obvious next thing that would pop into the reader's mind (Does it make sense?). Since that's roughly what you've stated as your Question, you can see that both it and the Answer match, so you have proved that the point you are making is valid for the reader.

6 Given the statement that the change does make sense, you can now move down to determine what *New Question* would be raised in the reader's mind by your stating it to him. (Why?)

7 The answer to any Why? question is always 'Reasons', so you know that the points you need across the Key Line must all be reasons. What might your reasons be?

- It will give us the information we need.

- It will increase our cash flow.

- It will reduce our work load.

8 After determining that in fact these points are the right points and in logical order, you can move down and spell out what you need to say to support each one. In the case of so short a document, however, you can probably get away with assuming they are easily available in your mind and will come to you as you get to each section to write it.

As you can see, the technique has forced the writer to draw from his mind only the information that will be relevant to the reader's question. But in doing so, it has helped push his thinking to deal fully with the question, rather than only partially as in the original example. And of course, if he follows the top-down order of presenting the ideas in writing, the entire message will be remarkably easy for the reader to absorb.

The bottom-up approach

There may be frequent occasions when you find that your thinking is not fully enough developed to work out the top part of the pyramid. Perhaps you can't decide precisely what your Subject is, or the Question isn't clear to you, or you can't sort out what the reader does and doesn't know for sure. In such cases, simply move down to the Key Line level.

If you can think of any Key Line points, fine; but often you won't be able to. Do not despair. You can work out the ideas from the bottom up by following a 3-step process.

1 List all the points you think you want to make.

2 Work out the relationships between them.

3 Draw conclusions.

Again, let me demonstrate how this technique would work by using a document that needs rewriting (Exhibit 7). This is a memorandum written

Exhibit 7 Original TTW Memorandum

To: Date: August 22, 2001
From: Subject: TTW

Following is a summary of the results of this last 2 weeks' work.

As we already knew composing costs are the most important part in all new settings ranging from 40 percent in Hardbacks to 50–55 percent in Paperbacks.

The most important elements in composing costs are:

Machine composition	30–50%
Reading	17–25%
First proof and revise	10–16%
Make up	10–20%
Imposition and plate laying	10–15%

A comparison with PAR standards shows that TTW has a relatively low productivity in composing. At the moment the composing estimators are working on some specific examples I have given to them.

Every job in composing goes through the same steps basically to ensure a high level of quality. This may explain partly why they are considered uncompetitive for composing simple jobs.

There is a good deal of interest in Aylesbury in finding out what are the facts behind their composing costs. I have spoken about it with Roy Walter, Brian Thompson and George Kennedy. Kennedy is willing to set up an experiment in order to find out: (1) if there are any steps in the composing process that can be eliminated, particulary for certain jobs, and (2) what are the causes behind the apparent low productivity – i.e., why do they rank below PAR.

Composing is at the present moment overloaded. Most of the jobs run behind schedule in the department. The present undercapacity is particularly acute in hand composition. TTW is paying lower wages than other printers in the area and it is becoming hard to get and retain compositors.

At the moment, they are faced with a new union demand. Also two compositors just left.

The department has less people than budgeted and their overtime hours exceed budget by more then 50 percent.

CONCLUSIONS

1. It seems feasible to reduce composing costs by:

   a. Simplifying the process for cheap jobs.
   b. Increasing productivity by changing methods.

2. In order to carry out the first one it would be necessary to do some experiments on specific jobs, following them throughout the whole process, and controlling the marginal effect on quality of changes in the number and timing of checks, and the customer's reaction to them. The savings involved could be up to 10 percent of total composing costs.

   The second way of reducing costs requires, I believe, detailed methods study. TTW ranks 20–50 percent below PAR in setting and hand composition and it seems it would be possible to do better than that.

3. A comparison between TTW and Baird, Purnell or Waterlow may throw some light on this. George Kennedy and Roy Walter seemed to be very interested in carrying out the comparison. I have told them it may not be very meaningful after all.

4. The attitudes with respect to composing costs in Aylesbury are mixed. Gerry Calvert feels that they are definitely high, George Kennedy claims that there is no hard evidence that they are and Roy Walter recognizes that for him they are a mystery. They all seem very willing to investigate them.

---

by a young consultant to his engagement manager after 2 weeks of working on his first assignment. The client was a printing company in England.

I know nothing about the situation or the subject other than what is stated in the memorandum. We therefore have to treat the document as a closed universe, withholding judgment on whether what he says is true or right. We just want to make what it says clear. The points he makes are listed in Exhibit 8. The next step is to work out their relationships to each other.

Go first to the recommendations, since it is always easier to determine the validity of action ideas than of situation ideas (see Chapter 9). What is the relationship between simplifying the process and changing the methods? None; they both say the same thing, so there is nothing to be gained by analyzing these.

Exhibit 8 TTW Analysis

Step 1: List the points

Problems
1. Low productivity in composing
2. Same steps for each job
3. Uncompetitive prices for simple jobs
4. Behind schedule
5. Paying lower wages
6. Shortage of people
7. High overtime
8. Below PAR in setting and hand composition

Solutions
1. Simplify the process for cheap jobs
2. Increase productivity by changing methods

Step 2: Work out the relationships

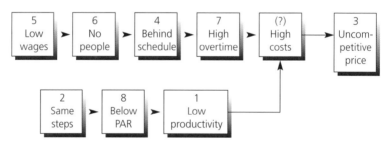

Step 3: Draw conclusions

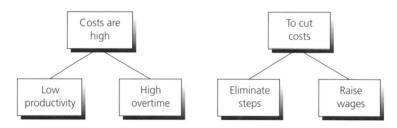

We move on to the problems, and in looking at them a moment, it becomes apparent that there are some cause-and-effect relationships implied here, which you want to lay out as visually as possible (Exhibit 8–Step 2). This analysis reveals two separate lines of reasoning, with the possibility that some points that should be made have been omitted.

Now you're ready to draw some conclusions. Either he's saying that the costs are high because the productivity is low and the overtime is high, or he's saying that to cut the costs you have to simplify the methods and raise the wages. To decide which, you want to think through the introduction. What does the original memo indicate the reader already knows?

Apparently he knows that costs are important, that TTW is uncompetitive in its pricing of simple jobs, and probably that nobody at TTW knows whether the costs are too high or not. In that case, your thinking might go something like this:

1 *Subject*	=	composing room costs.	
2 *Question*	=	are they too high?	
3 *Answer*	=	yes.	
4 *Situation*	=	composing room costs are the most important element in total cost.	
5 *Complication*	=	don't know if they are too high a proportion, but uncompetitiveness indicates they might be.	
Question (2)	=	are they too high?	
Answer (3)	=	yes.	
6 *New Question*	=	how do you cut them?	
7 *Key Line*	=	eliminate unnecessary steps in the composing process and raise wages to competitive levels.	

Exhibit 9 shows these ideas in what might have been an acceptable version of this memorandum. You may not agree with the young consultant's reasoning, but at least it is presented so clearly that the reader can determine whether he agrees with it or finds things to question about it.

I have reprinted the memorandum in full here because I want to demonstrate that the total introduction includes a statement of the Key Line points. With these included, the reader can get your entire thinking in the first 30 seconds or less of reading. And since the rest of the document exists only to explain or defend what you have already stated, he can be confident that no important points are going to jump up and surprise him later on. Consequently, he can scan if he has limited time available. Indeed, if your entire thinking is not clear to the reader in the first 30 seconds of reading, you should rewrite.

Exhibit 9 Rewritten TTW Memorandum

To: Date: August 22, 2001
From: Subject: TTW

I have spent the past 2 weeks in Aylesbury looking at costs in the
Composing Room. As we already knew, composing costs represent 40 percent of hardback costs, and 50–55 percent of paperbacks. TTW does not
know whether these costs are too high, but the company is considered
uncompetitive for simple jobs.

Our preliminary investigation indicates that composing costs could probably be cut considerably by:

- Eliminating unnecessary steps in the composing process
- Raising wages to competitive levels.

ELIMINATING STEPS

TTW ranks 20–50 percent below PAR standards in setting and hand composition. A look at composing methods shows that every job goes through
basically the same steps to ensure high quality, whether it is a Bible or a
thriller. This may explain partly why they are considered uncompetitive.

I have discussed these findings with Roy Walter, Brian Thompson, and
George Kennedy. Kennedy is willing to set up an experiment to learn (1)
whether any steps in the process can be eliminated, particularly for simple
jobs, and (2) the causes of the low PAR standing.

Beginning next week we will follow a few simple jobs through the
process, controlling the marginal effect on quality of changes in the number
and timing of checks, and test the customer's reaction to them. The savings
involved could be up to 10 percent of total composing costs. We will also
carry out a detailed methods study to try to close the PAR gap.

RAISING WAGES

TTW pays lower wages than other printers in the area, and is finding it difficult to get and retain compositors. Two compositors just quit, leaving the
department with fewer people than budgeted. As a result, most jobs are
running behind schedule, and overtime hours exceed budget by more than
50 percent.

The company presently faces a new union demand, which may force
them into higher wages. If so, they should be able to hire appropriate
people and eliminate the overtime charges.

In addition, the headings serve to highlight the major points of the structure so that the reader can quickly pick up the general thrust of your subordinate arguments if the document is a lengthy one. To this end, you want to take some care in the way you word the headings (see Chapter 6, *How to Highlight the Structure*), making sure to state them so that they reflect ideas, rather than categories. Never have a heading called 'Findings', for example, or 'Conclusion'. Such headings have no scanning value.

Caveats for beginners

It is clear that the rigidity of the pyramid rules enables you to start with an idea anywhere in the pyramid and discover all the others. Essentially, though, you will either be working from the top down or from the bottom up. I have tried to tell you exactly what to do in a general way, but the possibilities are endless, so that questions are inevitable. Following are the answers to some of the most commonly asked questions from beginning users of the pyramid.

1 *Always try top down first*. The minute you express an idea in writing, it tends to take on the most extraordinary beauty. It appears to have been chiseled in gold, making you reluctant to revise it if necessary. Consequently, never begin by just dictating the whole document 'to get it all down,' on the assumption that you can figure out the structure more easily afterwards. The chances are you'll love it once you see it typed, no matter how disjointed the thinking really is.

2 *Use the Situation as the starting point for thinking through the introduction*. Once you know what you want to say in the bulk of the introduction–Situation, Complication, Question, and Answer–you can place these elements in any order you like as you write, depending on the effect you want to create. The order you choose affects the tone of the document, and you will no doubt want to vary it for different kinds of documents. Nevertheless, begin your thinking with the Situation, since you're more likely to be able to think up the correct Complication and Question following that order.

3 *Don't omit to think through the introduction*. Very often you'll sit down to write and have the main point fully stated in your head, from which the Question is obvious. The tendency then is to jump directly down to the Key Line and begin answering the New Question raised by the statement of the main point. Don't be tempted. In most cases, you will find that you end up structuring

information that properly belongs in the Situation or Complication, and therefore forcing yourself into a complicated and unwieldy deductive argument. Sort out the introductory information first so that you leave yourself free to concentrate solely on ideas at the lower levels.

4 *Always put historical chronology in the introduction.* You cannot tell the reader 'what happened' in the body of the document, in an effort to let him know the facts. The body can contain only ideas, and ideas can relate to each other only logically. This means that you can talk about events only if you are spelling out cause-and-effect relationships, since these had to be discovered through analytical thinking. Simple historical occurrences do not exist as the result of logical thought, and therefore cannot be included as ideas.

5 *Limit the introduction to what the reader will agree is true.* The introduction is meant to tell the reader only what he already knows. Sometimes, of course, you won't know whether he actually knows something; at other times, you may be certain that indeed he does not know it. If the point being made can be easily checked by an objective observer and deemed to be a true statement, then your reader can be presumed to 'know' it in the sense that he will not question its truth.

6 *Be sure to support all Key Line points.* An idea has to be supported until you have answered all the questions likely to be raised by it. Naturally, not every point needs the same depth of support. At the Key Line level, however, all points must have at least one level of support. This is particularly true of the 'therefore' point in a deductive argument. If you find yourself with no need to support the final point, then you have overstructured your argument and probably need only an inductive grouping.

Fine points of introductions

4

As we saw in *How to Build a Pyramid Structure*, thinking through the introduction is the key step in discovering the ideas that must be presented in a document. By summarizing what the reader already knows, the introduction establishes the relevance of the question to which your document will give him the answer. You can then devote your energies to answering it.

However, actually finding the structure of the introduction can be a relatively complex and time-consuming activity. To this end, you may want a more comprehensive understanding of the theory and nature of initial introductions than was given earlier. You will also want some insight into the nature of the introductory comments needed at each of the key structural points in the body of the document.

Initial introductions

The initial introduction can be thought of as a circle around the top of your pyramid, outside the structure of the ideas you are presenting (Exhibit 10). It always tells the reader a story he already knows, in the sense that it states the Situation within which a Complication developed that raised the Question to which the document is giving the Answer. Why does it always have to be a story, and why one that he already knows?

Why a story?

If you think about it for a moment, you can accept that nobody really wants to read what you've written the way he *really* wants to read a novel that everyone has assured him is both gripping and sexy. He already has a multitude of jumbled and unrelated thoughts in his head, most of which are on other subjects, and all of which are very dear and interesting to him. To push these thoughts aside and concentrate only on the information you present, with no prior conviction of its interest to him, demands

Exhibit 10 Introductions should tell a story

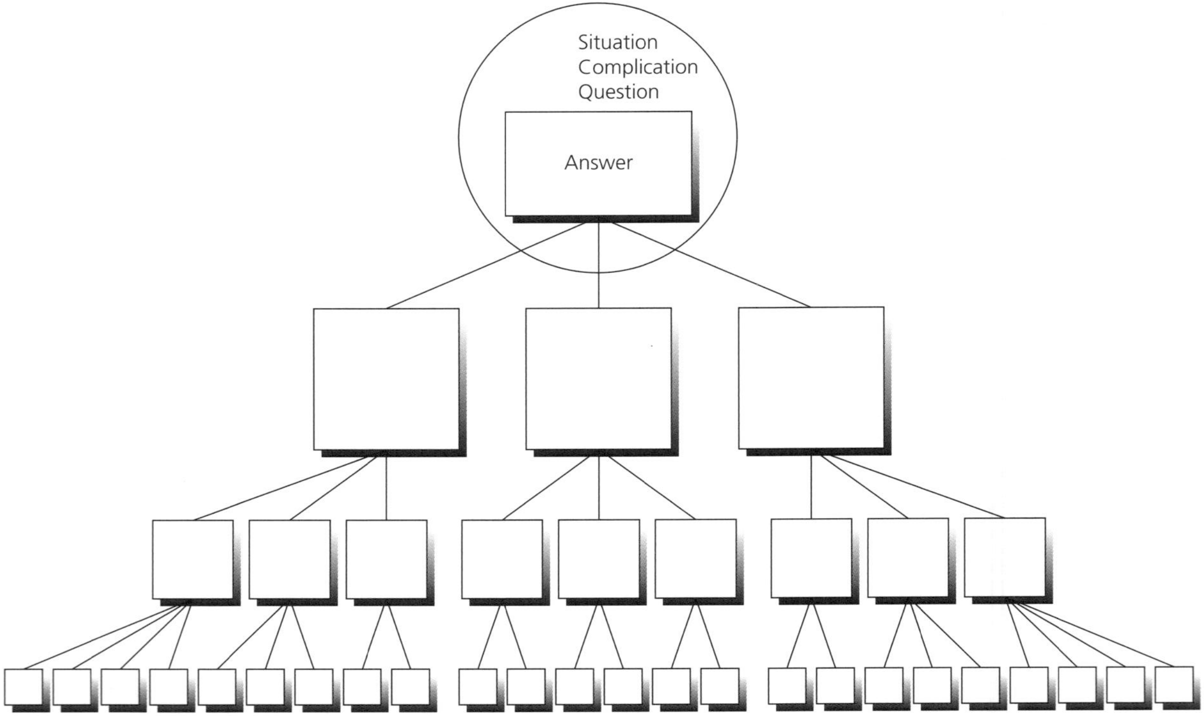

real effort. He will be pleased to make that effort only if there is a compelling enticement for him to do so.

Even if he is quite eager to know what your document contains, and convinced of its interest, he must still make the effort to push aside his other thoughts and concentrate on what you're saying. All of us have had the experience of reading a page and a half of something and suddenly realizing that we haven't comprehended a word. It's because we didn't push aside what was already in our heads.

Consequently, you want to offer the reader a device that will make it easy for him to push his other thoughts aside and concentrate only on what you're saying. A foolproof device of this sort is the lure of an unfinished story. For example, suppose I say to you:

> 'Two Irishmen met on a bridge at midnight in a strange city. . .'

I have your interest actively engaged for the moment, despite whatever else you may have been thinking about before you read the words. I have riveted your mind to a specific time and place, and I can effectively control where it goes by focusing it on what the two Irishmen said or did, releasing it only when I give the punch line.

That's what you want to do in an introduction. You want to build on the reader's interest in the subject by telling him a story about it. Every good story has a beginning, a middle, and an end. That is, it establishes a situation, introduces a complication, and offers a resolution. The resolution will always be your major point, since you always write either to resolve a problem or to answer a question already in the reader's mind.

But the story has also got to be a 'good' story for the reader. If you have any children you know that the best stories in the whole world are ones they already know. Consequently, if you want to tell the reader a really good story, you tell him one he already knows or could reasonably be expected to know if he's at all well informed.

Psychologically speaking, of course, this approach enables you to tell him things with which you know he will agree, prior to your telling him things with which he may disagree. Easy reading of agreeable points is apt to render him more receptive to your ideas than confused plodding through a morass of detail.

How long should it be?

How long should an introduction be? How long should a man's legs be? (Long enough to reach the ground.) The introduction should be long enough to ensure that you and the reader are 'standing in the same place' before you take him by the hand and lead him through your thinking.

Generally, this means two or three paragraphs, arranged as shown in Exhibit 11. The Situation and the Complication can each be as long as three or four paragraphs, but never more than that. It can't take very much to remind someone of what he already knows. Indeed, if you find yourself littering the introduction with exhibits, you can be sure that you are overstating the obvious.

By contrast, the introduction can also be as short as a sentence: 'In your letter of January 15 you asked me whether. . .' The closer you are in your everyday dealings to the person to whom you are writing, the shorter the introduction can get. But it must say enough to remind the reader of his Question.

Where do you start the situation?

You begin writing the Situation by making a statement about the subject that you know the reader will agree with because you are telling him something that he already knows. If you find you can't make a statement about the subject, then either you have the wrong subject, or you're starting in the wrong place to talk about it.

Exhibit 11 Set out the Key Line points at the beginning

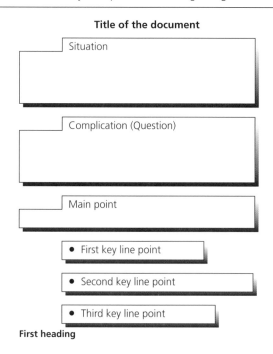

Title of the document

Situation

Complication (Question)

Main point

- First key line point
- Second key line point
- Third key line point

First heading

When you can readily identify the reader by name, as in a letter or memorandum, determining where to start is usually fairly straightforward. You start at the point where you can make a self-sufficient and noncontroversial statement about the subject – self-sufficient in the sense that no previous statement is needed to make the precise meaning of this one clear, and noncontroversial in the sense that you can expect him automatically to understand it and agree to it.

If you are writing a report for wide circulation, however, or a magazine article or a book, the job is not so much to remind the reader of the question as to plant one. Here getting started is a bit more difficult. Assume that your readers are moderately well informed, and present an explanation of what is already generally accepted knowledge on the subject. By arranging known material in a narrative form, and usually in a way that they haven't thought about it before, you inspire your readers to ask the question you wish to address.

The key characteristic of all opening Situation sentences is that they leave you expectant for further information – and that is what qualifies them to be openers. Each one establishes the base for a story to come. Here are some typical Situation opening sentences:

- Energoinvest is considering the possibility of exporting alumina from its Mostar plant to Ziar in Czechoslovakia. (Memorandum.)

- Every major health service is beset by increasing pressure on already scarce resources – and the Irish Health Service is no exception. (Report.)

- If we accept the common usage of words, nothing can be more readily disproved than the old saw, 'You can't keep a good man down.' (Book.)

What's a complication?

The Complication of the introduction is not a complication in the everyday sense of the word; it is the Complication to the story. It describes an alteration to a stable situation, rather than a problem per se, although sometimes the alteration is a problem. Exhibit 12 shows several possible kinds of complications.

Exhibit 12 The Complication states an alteration to the Situation

SITUATION	COMPLICATION	QUESTION
Recognized stable Situation	Something went wrong	What do we do?
	Something could go wrong	How can we prevent it?
	Something changed	What should we do?
	Something could change	How should we react?
	Here's what you might expect to find in it	Do we find it?
	Here's someone with a different point of view	Who is right?
	In this situation we have three alternatives	Which one should we take?

To illustrate further, Exhibit 13 shows some introductions pulled at random from popular publications, along with an outline of their structures.

Why that order?

The situation-complication-solution form of the introduction is essential. However, the order of the parts can be varied to reflect the tone you want to establish in the document. Note how the tone changes slightly in each of these examples:

Exhibit 13 Some patterns of introduction

Marketing Myopia

Every major industry was once a growth industry. But some that are now riding a wave of growth enthusiasm are very much in the shadow of decline. Others which are thought of as seasoned growth industries have actually stopped growing. In every case the reason growth is threatened, slowed, or stopped is not because the market is saturated. It is because there has been a failure of management.

S = Many major industries have stopped growing or are threatened by decline

C – Assumption is that growth is threatened because market is saturated

Q – Is that a correct assumption?

Harvard Business Review

Cracking Japanese Markets

With the strong yen creating an increasingly competitive environment and Washington achieving a conspicuous lack of success in trade negotiations. Many executives in the United States and Europe have abandoned their search for new opportunities in the Japanese market. Frustration has set in as attempts to become 'insiders' have proved futile. Some companies have shifted their attention to emerging markets like China and India, but by ignoring Japan they are making a big mistake.

S = US/European companies frustrated with Japan

C – Have shifted attention to China/India

Q – Are they making a mistake?

New York Times

Visual Thinking in the Ice Age

For the first 2.5 million years of the archeological record, the only artifacts left by man were strictly utilitarian: stone tools. Then, about 35,000 years ago in Europe a dramatic turning point was reached. In addition to new kinds of stone tools, we find symbolic objects: the first adornments of the body, in the form of beads and pendants, and the first known attempts at painting and sculpture.

This cultural explosion occurred at the same time over large parts of western and eastern Europe. Why?

S = For 2.5 million years we had only stone tools

C – Then suddenly 35,000 years ago we get art all over Europe

Q – Why?

National Geographic

CONSIDERED: situation-complication-solution
In recent years, the Firm has billed dozens of clients large amounts of money for diversification work. However, as yet no one in the London Office can claim the magnum of champagne available to the first consultant who can demonstrate an acquisition or merger by a client that would not have happened without our efforts. Since our diversification work has increased by 40 percent in the past 5 years, the time is ripe for a Firm Development Project to determine how we can ensure that diversification studies do bring significant benefits to the clients we serve.

This memorandum outlines the major issues and hypotheses that should be resolved and tested during the project.

DIRECT: solution-situation-complication
Our first priority for a Firm Development Project should be one directed toward improving our ability to help clients diversify. In the London Office alone, our work in helping clients find acquisition and merger candidates has increased by 40 percent over the past 5 years. Yet we cannot point to a single acquisition or merger that would not have happened without our efforts.

This memorandum outlines. . .

CONCERNED: complication-situation-solution
To my knowledge, no one in the London Office has yet conducted a single diversification study for a client that has yielded demonstrable results beyond what he could have done for himself. This situation is startling, since our practice in this area over the past 5 years has grown by 40 percent. We cannot in conscience go on charging clients for work that does not yield significant benefits and maintain our high reputation. I suggest, therefore, that we conduct a Firm Development Project to determine how we can make diversification studies an area of our practice that is proven to bring significant benefit to clients.

The memorandum outlines. . .

What about the key line?

The Key Line not only gives the answer to the new Question raised by the statement of your Main Point, it also indicates the plan of the document. If it is a lengthy one, therefore, you will want to set the points out in the middle of the page as shown in Exhibit 11. You can then put a heading to represent the first point, and start writing (see Chapter 6, *How to Highlight the Structure*).

Setting the points out enables the reader to get your entire thinking in the first 30 seconds or so of reading. Since anything that follows will serve only to explain or defend these points, you have courteously put the reader in the position of being able to determine whether he needs to go on or is ready to accept your conclusions as they stand. In any case, he now knows what to expect and can read with a greater sense of ease.

If the document is a short one, with only a paragraph or two to support each section, you do not of course want to set out the points and then repeat them in headings. In such cases, use the points as topic sentences to your paragraphs and underline them so that they jump out at the reader.

Remember that the Key Line points should be expressed as ideas. It is not sufficient, for example, to write an introduction like the following:

This memorandum describes the project team approach to identifying and achieving significant profit improvements. It is organized in six sections as follows:

Background
Principles of project team approach
What project work is
How the program is organized
Unique benefits and specific results
Prerequisites for success.

Here the setout of the points is useless in the sense of conveying the message of the document to the reader. It simply forces on the reader a string of words that he can't put into perspective – mere excess baggage that wastes his time and delays his understanding.

As a rule of thumb, you never want to have a section labelled 'Background' (or 'Introduction') because the major point it expresses will not be on the same level of abstraction as the other points that follow. In the example above, of course, because the writer is writing about subjects instead of about ideas, the ideas likely to be behind the subjects will probably not form a clear argument, either inductive or deductive.

Indeed, one suspects that the ideas in the various sections are badly jumbled as they stand. For example, the 'Unique benefits and specific results' should probably be discussed under the 'Principles of project team approach,' and the 'Prerequisites for success' probably belong under 'How the program is organized.' Never write about categories, only about ideas.

Further examples

If you are beginning to think that it might be difficult to write a good introduction, you're right. More botches are made of introductions than of any other part of a person's writing. However, by reading enough examples you should get a sense of when an introduction sounds 'right,' and keep working at yours until they do.

LETTER

In his article 'Japanese Businessmen: The Yen Is Mightier Than the Sword,' James Sterba credits the Sony Corporation with leading the way in commercial exploitation of the transistor while the inventor, Bell Telephone Laboratories, 'didn't know what to do with it except sell it to the Pentagon.'

The statement is neither descriptive truth nor objective metaphor. Bell Laboratories knew what to do with the transistor before the device was invented.

NEWSPAPER ARTICLE

The Nixon Administration has launched a phony attack on the television networks, and the networks have responded with a bogus defense. Uninstructed people, as a result, have the impression that freedom and liberty are under serious fire in this country.

In fact the issue is what kind of society we want to shape through television. It is a question of whether we want a self-indulgent society with anarchic tendencies, or a society of tighter common bonds including a touch of elitist culture.

REPORT

Adequate supplies of cheap phosphorus are the key to maximizing Greenwalt's profits, since phosphorus and its derivatives account for 75 percent of the company's sales and profits. However, a stable source of cheap phosphorus will not be available until 1996, when the Newfoundland plant comes on-stream. In the interim the high cost of United Kingdom production will adversely affect the company's profit levels.

Given that few major opportunities are likely from non-phosphorus-based business, it is necessary to review our phosphorus position, to ascertain whether anything further can be done to reduce substantially the cost of this material until the end of 1992. Examination indicates that a considerable profit opportunity is available to us. Achieving these savings is the subject of this report.

ESSAY*

The world has been slow to realize that we are living this year (1930) in the shadow of one of the greatest economic catastrophes of modern history. But now that the man in the street has become aware of what is happening, he, not knowing the why and the wherefore, is as full today of what may prove excessive fears as, previously, when the trouble was first coming on, he was lacking in what would have been a reasonable anxiety.

He begins to doubt the future. Is he now awakening from a pleasant dream to face the darkness of facts? Or dropping off into a nightmare which will pass away? He need not be doubtful. The other was not a dream; this is a nightmare, which will pass away with the morning.

For the resources of nature and men's devices are just as fertile and productive as they were. The rate of our progress toward solving the material problems of life is not less rapid. We are as capable as before of affording for everyone a high standard of life – high, I mean, compared with, say, 20 years ago – and will soon learn to afford a standard higher still.

We were not previously deceived. But today we have involved ourselves in a colossal muddle, having blundered in the control of a delicate machine, the working of which we do not understand. The result is that our possibilities of wealth may run to waste for a time – perhaps for a long time.

* Keynes, J.M., *Essays in Persuasion* (The Royal Economic Society, 1972).

BOOK*

In the second century of the Christian Era, the empire of Rome comprehended the fairest part of earth, and the most civilized portion of mankind. The frontiers of that extensive monarchy were guarded by ancient renown and disciplined valour.

The gentle, but powerful, influence of laws and manners had gradually cemented the union of the provinces.

Their peaceful inhabitants enjoyed and abused the advantage of wealth and luxury. The image of free constitution was preserved with decent reverence. The Roman Senate appeared to possess the sovereign authority, and devolved on the emperors all the executive powers of government.

During a happy period of more than fourscore years, the public administration was conducted by the virtue and abilities of Nerva, Trajan, Hadrian, and the two Antonines. It is the design of this and of the two succeeding chapters to describe the prosperous condition of their empire; and afterwards, from the death of Marcus Antoninus, to deduce the most important circumstances of its decline and fall: a revolution which will ever be remembered, and is still felt by the nations of the earth.

* Gibbon, Edward, *Decline and Fall of the Roman Empire.*

LONG-TERM PUBLISHING PROJECT*

A

Weekly Review

OF THE

Affairs of *FRANCE:*

Purg'd from the Errors and Partiality of *Newf-Writers* and *Petty-Statefmen*, of all Sides.

Saturday, Feb. 19. 1704.

The INTRODUCTION.

THIS Paper is the Foundation of a very large and ufeful Defign, which, if it meet with fuitable Encouragement, *Permiffu Superiorum*, may contribute to Setting the Affairs of *Europe* in a Clearer Light, and to prevent the various uncertain Accounts, and the Partial Reflections of our Street-Scriblers, who Daily and Monthly Amufe Mankind with Stories of Great Victories when we are Beaten, Miracles when we Conquer, and a Multitude of Unaccountable and Inconfiftent Stories, which have at leaft this Effect, That People are poffeft with wrong Notions of Things, and Nations Wheedled to believe Nonfenfe and Contradiction.

These examples demonstrate that the length of an introduction is not necessarily related to the length of the writing to follow. Rather, it is related to the needs of the reader. What does he have to be told not only to comprehend fully the significance of your main point, but also to want to read on to learn how you arrived at it?

In summary

I hope this discussion of opening introductions has made you think that it is important to devote a good deal of thought to ensuring that you write a good introduction. For as you can gather from the examples, a good introduction does more than simply gain and hold the reader's interest. It influences his perceptions.

The narrative flow lends a feeling of plausibility to the writer's particular interpretation of the situation, which by its nature must be a biased selection of the relevant details; and this feeling of plausibility constricts the reader's ability to interpret the situation differently. It also gives a sense of inevitable rightness to the logic of the writer's conclusion, making the reader less inclined to argue with the thinking that follows. Finally, it establishes the writer's attitude to the reader as a considerate one of wanting him clearly to understand the situation – to see behind the language to the reality it represents.

To emphasize the theory behind writing good introductions:

1 *Introductions are meant to remind rather than to inform.* This means that nothing should be included that would have to be proved to the reader for him to accept the statements of your points – i.e., no exhibits.

2 *They should always contain the three elements of a story.* These are the Situation, the Complication, and the Solution. And in longer documents you will want to add an explanation of what is to come. The first three elements need not always be placed in classic narrative order, but they do always need to be included, and they should be woven into story form.

3 *The length of the introduction depends on the needs of the reader and the demands of the subject.* Thus, there is scope to include whatever is necessary for full understanding: history or background of the problem, outline of your involvement in it, any earlier investigations you or others have made and their conclusions, definitions of terms, and statements of admissions. All these items can and should be woven into the story, however.

Some common patterns

As time goes on and you find yourself thinking through the introductions to a variety of documents, you will notice some common patterns begin to emerge. Which patterns will become common for you will, of course, depend on the business you are in. But to show you what I mean, here are the five patterns I have seen repeated most often, drawn from both business and consulting. They are:

1 Directives
2 Requests for funds
3 'How to' documents
4 Letters of Proposal
5 Progress Reviews

Directives

This must be the most common kind of business memorandum written anywhere in the world – reflecting a situation in which you are writing to tell someone else to do something. In this case, you will be planting the question in the reader's mind, rather than reminding him of it.

To illustrate, suppose you are holding a meeting for your field salesmen, at which you are planning to teach them how to present a new selling technique to chain grocery stores. However, in order to do so effectively you need some information from them on a particular problem chain in their local area. How would you structure the introduction? Very much in this manner:

S = At the field sales meeting we want to teach you how to present the Space Management Program
C = Need a profile of a problem chain in your area
Q = (How do I prepare the profile?)

Or, to put it as starkly as possible:

S = We want to do X
C = We need you to do Y
Q = How do I do Y?

In this case the question would be implied rather than stated, since the flow of the writing would not require it to be spelled out. Nevertheless, it is absolutely essential that you spell it out for yourself before you begin to write. Otherwise, you run the danger of not being absolutely sure of your question.

In this example, the question is 'How?' Whenever the question is 'How?' the answer is inevitably 'steps,' so that you would end up with a structure something like that shown in Exhibit 14. Note also that the Complication and the Answer are reversals of each other, since the Answer is the effect of carrying out the actions, which of course would solve the problem.

To try another example, suppose you have a procedures manual that various people in the company update or add to, and you want to make sure they all do it in the same way:

S = We have a manual covering activities where nonconformity of action would be detrimental. From time to time needs updating.
C = To ensure compatibility, important to follow the same procedure.
Q = (What is the procedure?)

And again you have another question that would be implied rather than stated in writing. To show the pattern starkly:

S = You do X
C = Must do in Y way
Q = What is Y way?

Requests for funds

Another very common memorandum type is one requesting funds. For

Exhibit 14 Field Sales Meeting

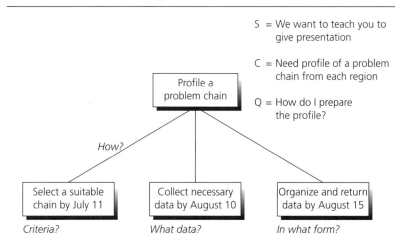

S = We want to teach you to give presentation

C = Need profile of a problem chain from each region

Q = How do I prepare the profile?

Profile a problem chain

How?

Select a suitable chain by July 11

Collect necessary data by August 10

Organize and return data by August 15

Criteria?

What data?

In what form?

those the reader's Question is always 'Should I approve the request?' and here again the Question would be implied rather than stated, as would the Complication. That is, you would have a formal structure that said:

S = The Consumer Group wishes to purchase a Wang System 25 II, together with four CRTs and three printers, at a cost of $___.
C = (They cannot purchase without your approval)
Q = (Should I approve?)

Only the Situation would be stated in the writing, and then the pyramid structure would tell the reader to approve the purchase for some set of relevant reasons.

For example:

We should approve this request because:

The cost will be more than offset by the projected savings
It will greatly increase the Group's productivity
It will create new opportunities for service.

'How to' documents

Frequently, particularly in consulting, you write because someone has a problem and you are telling him how to solve it. The structure of any 'how to' document is 'steps,' as shown below:

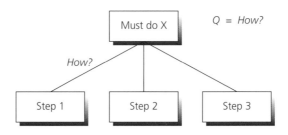

However, the introductory structure varies slightly depending on whether you are telling the reader how to do something he has not done before or whether you are telling him how to do properly what he is already doing. The memorandum on The Role of the Board shown on page 19 in Chapter 2 is an example of the first type:

S = Must do X activity
C = Not set up to do so
Q = How do we get set up?

By contrast, suppose you have a company whose market forecasting system gives inaccurate forecasts, and they want you to tell them how to make it give accurate ones. The structure is always:

S = Your present system is X
C = It doesn't work properly
Q = How change to make it work properly?

The trick here is to begin your thinking by literally laying out the present process as they do it now. (See Exhibit 15.) Then lay out the process as you think it should be done. The differences between the first structure and the second tell you what the steps on your Key Line must be.

Exhibit 15 Comparison of Processes

Present process

Recommended process

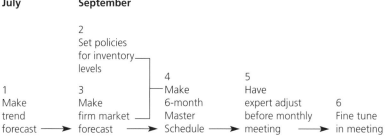

Recommended process

Let me emphasize the importance of making the two processes visible to yourself before you begin to write. You may assume that you know precisely what they are, having been working on them for so long. But unless you lay them out and compare them, the chances of leaving something important out are very great. You cannot be sure your thinking is complete and that you have not left anything out unless you make the actual step-by-step comparison. I have seen many examples of incomplete thinking in this area that I make a special point of mentioning it. Indeed, we had an example in the Big Chief memo in Chapter 3.

Letters of proposal

These documents are the lifeblood of consulting, and have thus had a good deal of thought lavished on them over the years by consulting firms. Most firms follow this approach:

S = You have a problem
C = You have decided to bring in an outsider to solve it
Q = (Are you the outsider we should hire to solve it?)

The Answer to the Question is always 'yes,' of course, followed by a 3-part structure explaining that:

1 We understand the problem

2 We have a sound approach for solving it

3 We have good people to work on it.

This is perfectly logical in concept. However, let me point out that, structurally, the only section that reflects thinking is the approach section. The first section is an extended description of the Situation, playing back to the reader in organized form everything he has told you about how the problem arose. Similarly, the final section, while true, is simply a listing of the qualifications of the people who will be assigned to the team.

The major thinking is done in the approach section, where you specify the steps you will take (never more than 5) to solve the problem. These steps must be stated in end-product terms as explained in Chapter 9, and will serve to define the major phases of the study, with the specific end products to be expected at the end of each phase. It is on the basis of the approach that the client should make his decision to hire, although alas that is not always the case.

Progress reviews

Finally we come to Progress Reviews. These are usually the formal com-munications one schedules with the client at the end of each phase of the study, leading up to the final report. After the first one, the structure is always the same.

The first one will say something like this:

S = You people have X problem.
C = We told you in our Letter of Proposal that we would do Y first to solve it. We have now done Y.
Q = What did you find?

Once this presentation has been made, the client will have a particular reaction. Perhaps he will ask you to investigate an anomaly you have uncovered in your work. Or he may approve what you've done and tell you to move on to phase two. At the time of your next progress review, then, you might say something like this:

S = In our last progress review we told you that you had a capacity problem
C = You said you thought this would not be a problem long because you believed your competition was shortly going out of business. You asked us to investigate whether that were the case. We have now completed our investigation.
Q = (What did you find?)
A = We found that you will still have a capacity problem, only worse.

Or to put it in skeletal form:

S = We told you X
C = You asked us to investigate Y, which we have done
Q = What did you find?

What must be apparent by now from these examples is that the pivot on which your entire document depends is the Question, of which there is always only one to a document. If you have two, they must be related: 'Should we enter the market, and if so, how?' is really 'How should we enter the market?' since if the answer to the first question is no, the second question is not dealt with.

On occasion you will not be able to determine the question easily just by thinking through the introduction. In that case, look at the material you intend to include in the body. Whenever you have a set of points you want to make, you want to make them because you think the reader should know them. Why should he know them? Only because they answer a question. Why would that question have arisen? Because of his situation. So that by working backward you can invent a plausible introduction to give your question a logical provenance.

Transitions between groups

Once you have written your introduction and moved into the body of your document, you must pause periodically to let the reader know where you've been and where you next plan to go – at either the end or the beginning of each major grouping. In doing so, however, you want to make your progress from point to point seem smooth and nonmechanical. Thus, you do not want to say such things as:

> This chapter has looked at the need for priorities. The next chapter looks at how these priorities should be set.

In other words, you do not want to relate what two chapters or sections *do*, you want to relate what they say – their major ideas. And you want to do it in such a way that you seem to be looking in two directions at once – back to what has been said and forward to what is to be said. If you make this pause at the beginning of a chapter, section, or subsection, you should use the technique of referencing backward. If the chapters or sections are long ones, then you will probably find it clearer to pause at the end and make a summary before going on.

Referencing backward

The technique of referencing backward consists simply of picking up a word or a phrase or the main idea of the preceding portion of the pyramid that you are linking, and using it in your opening sentence. You are probably familiar with the technique in transitions between paragraphs. For example:

> No single executive has full-time responsibility for directing Group affairs. The absence of necessary leadership and coordination for senior operating and staff executives results in . . . (list of problems).
>
> The problems stemming from *lack of full-time leadership* are compounded by overlapping or unwieldy responsibility assignments …

You follow precisely the same technique at the beginning of a new chapter, a new major section, or a new subsection. Suppose you had just finished a chapter telling the Ritz-Ryan hotel chain that it was not taking full advantage of its common ownership of many hotel, restaurant, and catering operations. You are about to start a new chapter outlining the changes that would have to be made in the top executive structure if the Group is to be in a position to take advantage, and you have a pyramid like that shown opposite. Your linkings, referencing backward, might read as follows:

Between the chapters
The current top executive and board structure suffers from two major shortcomings that severely limit the degree to which Ritz-Ryan can *take advantage of its combined resources*.

Between the two major sections
In addition to appointing a Group Managing Director, a number of changes should be made in the executive structure to establish short, clear lines of authority and responsibility.

Between the first two subsections
Just as only a full-time Chief Executive can *coordinate line and staff activities effectively*, so only a full-time Chief Executive can provide the steady, strong and relentless pressure needed to bring about improvements throughout the organization.

I'm sure you see the technique. The point is to make the transitions unobtrusive yet clear, primarily through picking up the key word or phrase and carrying it forward. You are, of course, carrying it forward to connect with the major point of the next section, which has already been introduced briefly in the 'explanation' part of your original introduction. Thus, here you need not lead up to it with a 'story' as you did previously, since your reader now presumably has as much information as he needs to understand the points. You do, however, need to introduce the grouping of ideas to come under this section, and explain how they support its major point.

Exhibit 16 Ritz-Ryan Example

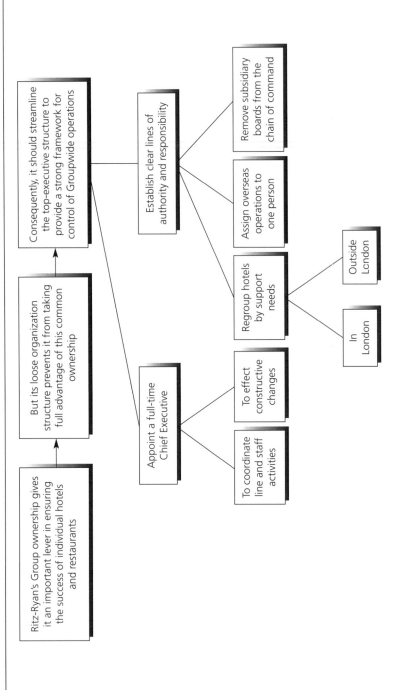

Summarizing

Sometimes the chapter or section will be extremely long or complicated, in which case you will want to stop and summarize completely before going on. An example of doing this is at the end of the first section on page 49, where the conclusions about introductions are summarized. Here is the summary that appeared at the end of the Ritz-Ryan chapter we have just been discussing.

> In summary, the top-level executive structure recommended in this chapter consists of the Ritz-Ryan Board and Chairman, a Group Managing Director, and three key executives reporting to him, each in charge of one of the Group's major businesses. These positions and reporting relationships provide a strong framework for long-term leadership and control of Groupwide operations. Only by streamlining the structure to provide this degree of control and accountability can the Group realize the improvement of opportunities identified elsewhere in this report.

Concluding summaries of this sort are not difficult to write if you keep in mind that they are meant to restate, as adroitly as possible, the principal matter and tone of the preceding text. Since you have these in front of you in your pyramid, all you are doing is pulling them together again for the reader.

In all of this positioning, the intention is to make the job of thinking required of the reader as easy as possible. He is, after all, rarely trained in analysis and reflection, and can have nowhere near the understanding of the subject you have even if the subject is his own company. You and he are not peers in interpreting your thinking on the subject.

Thus, you must expect that his mind will not be precisely where you want it to be, in terms of understanding, as you finish one lengthy group of points and prepare to go on to the next. Your transitions are meant to grab his mind, as it were, and pull it back to where it belongs if he is to comprehend what you are trying to say. This is essentially an exercise in good manners, provided it is done gracefully and only where needed.

Concluding

Theoretically, if you write a proper introduction and structure the body of your document to obey the pyramid rules, you should not need a concluding statement. You have, after all, clearly stated your reader's question at the beginning, and answered it fully with impeccable logic.

Nevertheless, you may feel a psychological need to end gracefully rather than simply to stop writing. The tendency to end short memos by saying, 'If you have any further questions, please do not hesitate to call,' no doubt reflects this need.

The obvious, perhaps too obvious, procedure at the end of a longer document is to signal the end by putting a line of asterisks in the middle of the page, which is sometimes called a 'sunset.' You then begin your last paragraph with the words, 'In conclusion …' and re-emphasize your main point. However, if you favour this approach you want to avoid merely making a lame restatement of what you have already made abundantly clear:

> This report has outlined our recommendations for reorganizing the company and spelled out the specific steps each department must take to bring it about.'

Rather, you want to find a compelling set of words that not only sums up for the reader what you have been saying, but also produces an appropriate emotion in him about it. At least, that is Aristotle's advice about what to do in a conclusion.

That there is an 'appropriate emotion' for the end of a business document may be open to question, but I should think the major feeling you want to leave with your reader is that of a need and desire to act. Consequently, you want to give him some indication of what he is to think about or is able to do with the new knowledge he now possesses as a result of his reading. This can take the form of either a philosophical insight or a prescription for immediate action. Abraham Lincoln, in his second inaugural address, managed to do both:

> 'With malice towards none, with charity for all, with firmness in the right, as God gives us to see the right, let us strive on to finish the work we are in – to bind up the nation's wounds – to care for him who shall have borne the battle, and for his widow and his orphan – to do all which may achieve and cherish a just and lasting peace among ourselves and with all nations.'

You will, of course, want to be as subtle and restrained as your subject and your reader demand, so that what is an appropriate ending will vary with each. An airline president, for example, would probably be offended by strongly emotional statements when being urged to adopt a new planning system. But on a subject on which he already feels strongly, such as deregulation of his industry, he would surely be wide open to emotional appeals.

In general, however, if you insist on appending a conclusion, you will want to write something that puts into perspective the significance of your message. Here, for example, is the concluding paragraph of a report whose message was that it is technically possible to create a European-wide system for rapid retrieval by computer of technical literature.

'If you succeed in launching the system, you will not just have created the means for improved access to scientific and technical information in Europe by users in industry, commerce, the professions, and academia. You will also have created a common market for information, one that makes available the full range of existing sources, not just national collections, to all users. This could lead not only to advances in standardization and harmonization, but also to the development of totally new standards. We find the prospect exciting, and are eager to work with you in launching the pilot project.'

As you may have gathered from my tone, I do not encourage most people to write concluding paragraphs because they are so difficult to do well. Simple pragmatism dictates that you do without. However, there is an occasion on which you will definitely need a concluding section, and that is when you are dealing with future actions.

Sometimes you will write a very long document that recommends a course of action that you think the reader is likely to take. If he takes it, there are some things he ought to do Monday morning to get things in motion. To house these activities, you create a section called *Next Steps*. The only rule is that what you put in this section must be something that the reader will not question. That is, activities must be logically obvious ones.

For example, suppose you are recommending that the client buy a company, and you think that he is going to do so. After 30 pages of explaining why you think it is a good idea, you assume you have him convinced. You then title your next section *Next Steps*, and say something like, 'If you think this is a good buy then you should:

- Call the man who owns it and ask him to lunch.
- Call the bank to make sure the money for purchase will be available when you need it.
- Reconvene the Acquisitions Committee to handle the administrative details.

Clearly, your reader is not going to say to you, 'Why do I ask him to lunch, why can't I ask him to dinner?' These are self-evident points, and can be accepted without demur. If, on the other hand, they were points that did raise questions in his mind, then you would have to include them in the body of your text, and make certain they fit horizontally and vertically with everything else you're saying.

Deduction and induction: the difference

As we have demonstrated, clear writing results from a clear exposition of the exact relationships between a group of ideas on the same subject. Properly organized, these ideas will always form a pyramid, with the various levels of abstraction sorted out and related under a single thought.

Ideas in the pyramid relate in three ways – up, down, and sideways. An idea above a grouping summarizes the ideas below, while these ideas in turn explain or defend the point above. At the same time, the ideas in the grouping march sideways in logical order. What constitutes logical order differs depending on whether the pyramided group was formed deductively or inductively.

These two forms of reasoning are the only patterns available for establishing logical relationships between ideas. Consequently, an understanding of how they differ and what their rules are is essential to being able to sort out your thinking and express it clearly in writing.

Briefly, the difference is as shown in Exhibit 17. Deduction presents a line of reasoning that leads to a 'therefore' conclusion, and the point above is a summary of that line of reasoning, resting heavily on the final point. Induction defines a group of facts or ideas to be the same kind of thing, and then makes a statement (or inference) about that sameness. The deductive points derive from each other; the inductive points do not.

These differences are really quite enormous, as the next two sections will demonstrate. Once you have digested them, you should have little difficulty in recognizing or sorting out either form of reasoning, or in choosing the one that appropriately permits you to say clearly what you mean.

Deductive reasoning

Deductive reasoning appears to be the pattern the mind generally prefers to use in most of its thinking, possibly because it is easier to construct than inductive reasoning. In any case, it is usually the pattern one follows in problem solving, and therefore the one

Exhibit 17

Deductive reasoning

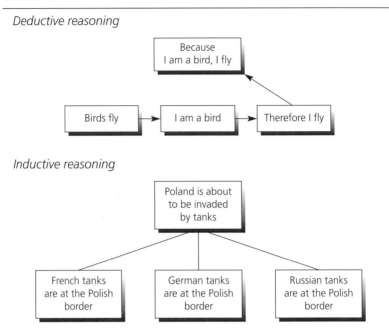

Inductive reasoning

people attempt to follow in communicating their thinking. But while it is a useful way to think, it is a ponderous way to write, as I shall hope to show.

How it works

First, let's understand what deductive reasoning is. It is usually described as taking the form of a syllogism – an argument in which a conclusion is inferred from two premises, one major and one minor. I find these terms confusing in explaining how deductive thinking works in writing, and so I will not use them again.

Instead, think of a deductive argument as needing to do three things:

- Make a statement about a situation that exists in the world.
- Make another statement about a related situation that exists in the world at the same time. The second statement relates to the first if it comments on either its subject or its predicate.
- State the implication of these two situations existing in the world at the same time.

Exhibit 18 shows several deductive arguments, each of which can be seen to do precisely these three things. And in each case the point at the top should roughly summarize the ideas grouped below, resting heavily on the final point. Thus, 'Because Socrates is a man he is mortal,' or 'Since the

Exhibit 18 Examples of deductive arguments

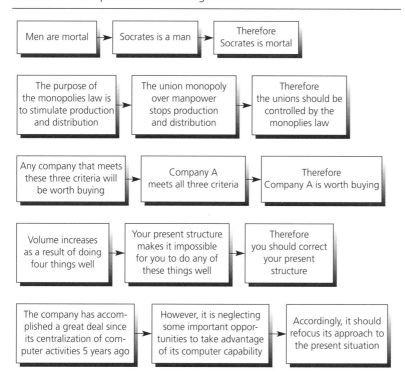

unions behave as a monopoly, they should be controlled by the monopolies law,' or 'If you want to increase your volume, you must correct your present structure,' and so forth.

These are examples of deductive arguments in which each step of the reasoning has been included. But sometimes you will find yourself wanting to skip a step and chain two or more deductive arguments together, since to put in every step would take too long and sound pedantic. This chaining of arguments is perfectly permissible, provided that your reader is likely to grasp and agree with the missing steps. Exhibit 19 gives an example of a chained deductive argument that should probably go something like this:

We produce enough used newspaper to meet our own demand.

But we have done more than meet our own demand.

Therefore we have a shortage.

A shortage of used newspaper causes a shortage of newsprint.

We have a shortage of used newspaper.

Therefore we have a shortage of newsprint.

Exhibit 19 Examples of a chained deductive argument

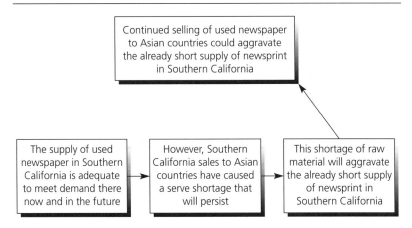

You can see how boring this argument would be to read if you put in every step, and in general that is my major complaint about the use of deductive arguments in writing. They are boring, primarily because they make a mystery story out of what should be a straightforward point.

When to use it

This leads me to urge that, on the Key Line level, you try to avoid using a deductive argument, and strive instead always to present your message inductively. Why? Because it is easier on the reader.

Let's look at what you force the reader to do when you ask him to absorb a deductively organized report. Suppose you wish to tell him that he must change in some way. Your argument would look something like this:

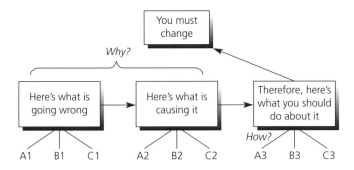

To absorb your reasoning, the reader must first take in and hold the A-B-Cs of what is going wrong. I agree this is not a difficult task, but then you ask him to take the first A of what is going wrong, bring it over and relate it to the second A of what is causing it, and then hold *that* in his head while you make the same match for the Bs and Cs. Next you ask him to repeat the process, this time tying the first A of what is going wrong to the second A of what is causing it, and hauling the whole cartload to hitch to the third A of what to do about it. And the same with the Bs and Cs.

Not only do you make the reader wait a very long time to find out what he should do Monday morning, you also force him to re-enact your entire problem-solving process before he receives his reward. It is almost as if you're saying to him, 'I worked extremely hard to get this answer, and I'm going to make sure you know it.' How much easier on everybody were you simply to present the same message inductively:

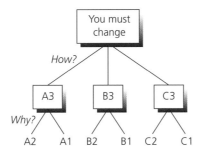

Here, instead of answering the 'Why?' question first and the 'How?' question second, you simply reverse the order. And now, while you may indeed have deductive arguments at the lower levels, still you have answered the reader's major question directly, with clear fences in your thinking between subject areas, and all information on each subject in one place.

To explain it another way, at the end of the problem-solving process, you will have come up with a set of ideas that can be sorted onto a Recommendation Worksheet like that shown in Exhibit 20. This permits you to visualize the fact that you have gathered findings that led you to draw conclusions from which you determined recommendations.

In writing to recommend action, you will never give findings that do not lead to conclusions, nor state conclusions that are not based on findings. (The conclusions are, in fact, the findings at a higher level of abstraction.) Nor will you have conclusions that do not lead to recommendations, nor recommendations that are not based on conclusions. (One conclusion can lead to several recommendations, and several conclusions can lead to one recommendation, but there must always be a connection.)

The conclusions generally state the problem that the recommendations solve. Consequently, the effect of the recommendation is to solve the problem you concluded was there. For example, sales are off 40 percent (finding) because our competitor added a new device to his product

Exhibit 20

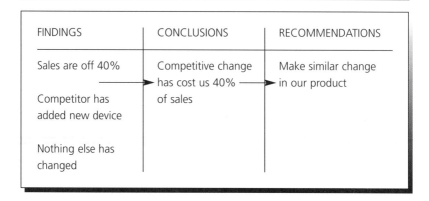

FINDINGS	CONCLUSIONS	RECOMMENDATIONS
Sales are off 40%	Competitive change has cost us 40% of sales	Make similar change in our product
Competitor has added new device		
Nothing else has changed		

(conclusion as to why sales are off), so you recommend that we add a similar device to ours. The effect of the recommendation is to make our product competitive.

Now, you can present this message deductively, one column at a time, in effect:

- Sales are off 40%.
- They are off because of competitive changes.
- Therefore, I recommend we make similar changes.

Or you can simply turn the whole thing 90 degrees to the left and begin with the recommendation:

We must redesign to regain position
   Competition has done so
   Has resulted in a 40% loss of our market share.

The issue here is whether it is better to tell the reader why he should change and then how to go about it, or that he should change and why. As a rule of thumb, it is always better to present the action before the argument, since that is what the reader cares about, unless you face one of those rare cases in which it is the argument he really cares about. I can think of only two situations in which the argument might be more important to the reader than the action:

- If he is going to disagree strongly with your conclusion, so you must prepare him to accept it.
- If he is incapable of understanding the action without prior explanation (as in a paper on how to do risk analysis), so that you must give him the reasoning that underlies it.

Few of the recipients of business documents fall into either class, however, so that in general you will find yourself wanting to structure the Key Line of your pyramid to form an inductive argument.

Note that I am talking only about the Key Line here, and not about lower levels. Deductive arguments are very easy to absorb if they reach you directly:

When, however, you must plough through 10 or 12 pages between the first point and the second, and between the second and the third, then they lose their instant clarity. Consequently, you want to push deductive reasoning as low in the pyramid as possible, to limit intervening information to the minimum. At the paragraph level deductive arguments are lovely, and present an easy-to-follow flow. But inductive reasoning is always easier to absorb at higher levels.

Inductive reasoning

Inductive reasoning is much more diffi-cult to do well than is deductive reasoning, since it is a more creative activity. In inductive reasoning the mind notices that several different things (ideas, events, facts) are similar in some way, brings them together in a group, and comments on the significance of their similarity.

In the example of the Polish tanks cited in Exhibit 17, the events were all defined as warlike movements against Poland. Hence, the inference that Poland was about to be invaded. If, however, the events had been defined as preparations by Poland's allies to attack the rest of Europe, a quite different inference would have been in order.

This brings us to the two major skills one must develop to think cre-atively in the inductive form:

- Defining the ideas in the grouping
- Identifying the misfits among them.

How to do both things with precision is explained in considerable detail in Chapter 7. But at this point you need only understand the rudiments of how it is done to be able to distinguish the process from deduction.

How it works

The key technique is to find one word that describes the kind of ideas in your grouping. This word will always be a plural noun (a) because any 'kind of' thing will always be a noun, and (b) because you will always have more than one of the 'kind of' idea in your grouping. 'Warlike movements' is a plural noun in this sense, and so is 'preparations for attack.'

If you look at the inductive groupings in Exhibit 21, you will easily be able to see that each one can be described by a plural noun: schemes,

Exhibit 21 Clear inductive arguments

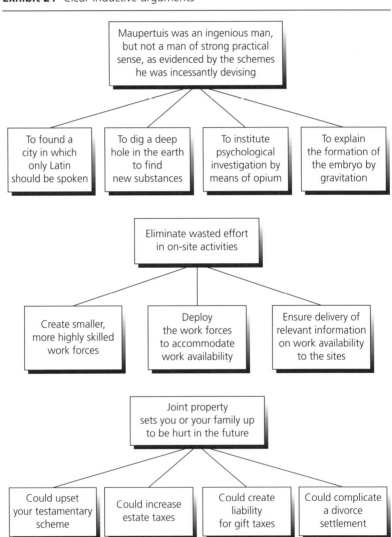

steps, ways of hurting. And in each case again you can see that none of the ideas in any of the three groupings is a misfit; each one matches the description of the plural noun.

The next step is always to check your reasoning, and this is done by questioning from the bottom up. For example, if you see a man who wants to found a city in which only Latin should be spoken, dig a deep hole in the center of the earth, etc., can you infer that this is an ingenious man, but not a man of strong practical sense? Yes, you can, or at least you could when the statement was originally written.

By contrast, consider the two examples in Exhibit 22. If you see managers who don't face reality, won't countenance criticism, etc., can you infer that they mismanage because they want to? Certainly not, it's sloppy reasoning and writing.

What about the next one? If productivity is low, overtime high, and prices uncompetitive, can you infer that you have a profit-improvement opportunity? Perhaps, but I can think of three or four other things that could also be labelled indicators of a profit-improvement opportunity. In that case, you know the overall point is at too high a level of abstraction in relationship to the three points grouped below, since it does not make a statement specifically and only about them.

Exhibit 22 Poor inductive arguments

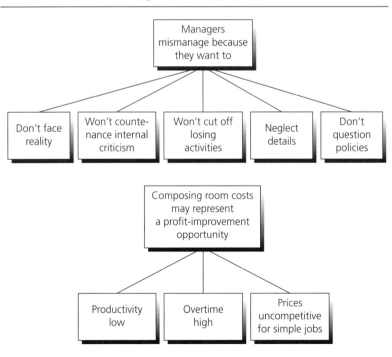

In fact, however, this is really a deductive argument masquerading as an inductive one, as you may have remembered from the example in Chapter 3. The low productivity led to the high overtime, which led to uncompetitive prices. Whenever you have only one piece of evidence for anything, you are forced to deal with it deductively. Thus, the point implied at the top is something like 'Our prices are high because our productivity is low.'

How it differs

I'm sure you can see now how very different deduction and induction are, and how easily you can tell the difference. Remember, if you are thinking deductively, your second point will always comment on the subject or predicate of the first. If it does not so comment, you should be able to classify it by the same plural noun as the first, to test that you have a proper inductive grouping.

To demonstrate, I recently ran across two so-called deductive fallacies in a logic book, which went as follows:

> All communists are proponents of socialized medicine
> Some members of the administration are proponents of socialized medicine.
> *Therefore some members of the administration are communists.*
>
> All rabbits are very fast runners.
> Some horses are very fast runners.
> *Therefore, some horses are rabbits.*

In both cases, I'm sure you will instantly be able to see that the second point does not make a comment on the first point, so these ideas cannot be deductively related. What the second point does do in each case is to add another member to the classification (plural noun) established in the first point. Placing ideas in classes is defining them by a plural noun, and you know that that is induction.

To test yourself, suppose I say to you:

> • Japanese businessmen are escalating their drive for the Chinese market.

Can you pick which of the next two points relates inductively to this, and which one deductively?

- The fact that American businessmen will soon be entering the market is sure to stimulate them further.
- American businessmen are escalating their drive for the Chinese market.

Clearly the first is deductive and the second inductive.

Note that with inductive ideas you generally either hold the subject constant and vary the predicate, or hold the predicate constant and vary the subject.

For example, you could say:

- Japanese businessmen are escalating their drive for the Chinese market
- American businessmen are escalating their drive for the Chinese market
- German businessmen are escalating their drive for the Chinese market

  The smart money is moving into China.

or you could say:

- Japanese businessmen are escalating their drive for the Chinese market
- Japanese businessmen are escalating their drive for the Indian market
- Japanese businessmen are escalating their drive for the Australian market

Japanese businessmen are moving aggressively into Southeast Asia.

It is interesting to note that whether you couple the ideas to form an inductive grouping or the beginning of a deductive line of reasoning, your mind automatically expects either a summarizing statement or a 'therefore' point. This expectation of the mind for deductive and inductive arguments to be completed often leads the reader to project his thinking ahead, to formulate what he thinks your next point will be. If his is different from yours, he can become both confused and annoyed. Consequently, you want to make sure that he will easily recognize the direction in which your thinking is tending by giving him the top point before you state the ideas grouped below.

How to highlight the structure

Once you have worked out the logic of your pyramid and are ready to begin writing, you want to be sure you arrange your ideas on the page in a way that emphasizes the various divisions of thought. In doing so, you will naturally reflect the hierarchical structure of the pyramid, as shown in Exhibit 23.

You can reflect this hierarchy in a variety of ways, the most common of which are headings, underlined points, decimal numbering, and indented display. Feelings run high about which of these is the 'best' formatting device. I myself lean to the use of headings as described below. However, in deference to what are excellent reasons given by proponents of the others, I discuss them as well.

Whichever format you choose, remember that your objective is to make comprehension easier for the reader. This means that the format must be applied properly to reflect the levels of abstraction in your argument. To give the desired appearance without the proper content can cause confusion.

To this end, you want to make sure you thoroughly understand the rules before you begin application.

Headings

Essentially, the technique is to place signs for increasingly subordinate ideas ever further to the right of the page (Exhibit 24). Thus, major ideas are capped with major section headings at the left-hand margin, divisions of these major ideas are capped with subsection headings, divisions of those with numbered paragraphs, and so on. Of course, the style of headings you choose need not necessarily follow this particular form, but whatever the form, each heading should represent a division of thought.

Because your headings will represent divisions of thought, their use should reflect the relationships between the ideas inherent in the pyramid. To this end, you will want to take care that you:

Exhibit 23 Headings should reflect the divisions of thought

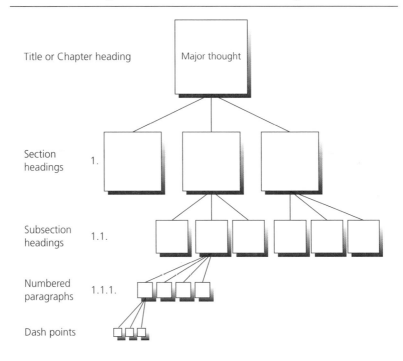

Title or Chapter heading — Major thought

Section headings — 1.

Subsection headings — 1.1.

Numbered paragraphs — 1.1.1.

Dash points

1 *Never use only one of any element.* Since the headings indicate levels of abstraction in the pyramid, you can never have only one item at each level. Thus, you can never have only one major section, or one subsection, or one numbered paragraph, or one dash point. Put more plainly, you shouldn't just stick in a heading because you think it would look good on a page, the way newspapers and magazines do, to break up the printing. A heading is meant to call attention to the fact that the idea it represents is one of a group, all of which are needed to understand the overall thought they support.

2 *Show parallel ideas in parallel form.* Since all of the ideas in a group are the same kind of idea, you want to emphasize this sameness by using the same grammatical form for the wording of each heading, etc. Consequently, if the first idea in a group of major section headings begins with a verb, all the rest must as well; if the first idea in a group of subsection headings begins with an 'ing' word, so should all the others:

Appoint a full-time Chief Executive
　　To coordinate activities
　　To effect improvements

Establish clear lines of authority
　　Regrouping hotels by support needs
　　Assigning responsibility for overseas operations
　　Removing Boards from the chain of command.

As you can see, because the subsection headings in the first group begin with the word 'To' does not necessarily mean that those in the second group must do so as well. Remember that there are invisible fences imposed between the ideas in each major section. Thus, the parallelism to be emphasized is between ideas in the subsection group, not between groups of subsections.

3 *Limit the wording to the essence of the thought.* The headings are meant to remind, not to dominate. Thus, you want to make them as concise as possible. You would not want, for example, to make the first major section heading above read 'Appoint a full-time Chief Executive to provide clear central authority.'

4 *Don't regard headings as part of text.* Headings are for the eye more then they are for the mind. As a result, they are not often read carefully, and you cannot depend on them to carry your message. Accordingly, you need to make sure that your opening sentence under a heading indicates that you are turning to a new topic. In fact, your entire document should be able to be read as a smooth-flowing piece without the headings. By the same token, you should never use the headings as part of the text.

For example:

Appoint a full-time Chief Executive
　　This action will go far toward clarifying the day-to-day responsibilities of …

This rule, of course, does not apply to numbered paragraphs, which are meant to be read as part of the text.

5 *Introduce each group of headings.* In doing so, you want to state the major point that the grouping will explain or defend, as well as the ideas to come. To omit this service is to present the reader with a mystery story, since he will then not be able to judge what the point is you are trying to make in that section until he gets to the end – and by then he may well have forgotten the beginning. For

Exhibit 24 Examples of Headings

---

1. THIS IS A CHAPTER HEADING

Chapter headings are numbered and centered, and should be worded to reflect the major thought to be developed in the chapter. The paragraphs immediately following a chapter heading (or title) should express the major idea clearly, as well as supply whatever other information the reader requires to ensure that you and he are 'standing in the same place' before you make your point and tell him how you plan to develop it. Subsequent chapter headings should be written in parallel style.

The major divisions of thought you plan to have may be set out with paragraph points or some other distinguishing mark:

- First major thought to come.
- Second major thought to come.

THIS IS A SECTION HEADING

The wording of section headings should also reflect the idea to be developed in the section to follow, and the wording of the first should parallel that of the others. A section can be further divided either into subsections or, if the points are short, into numbered paragraphs. The principal ideas of the subsections should be introduced and may be set off with paragraph points:

- First subthought to come.
- Second subthought to come.

This is a Subsection Heading

These, too, should be worded to reflect the principal thoughts they cover, and expressed in parallel style. If you wish further to divide the thought in a subsection, you can use numbered paragraphs.

1. **This is a numbered paragraph.** The first sentence or opening phrase can be underlined to highlight the similarity of the points being numbered. The point to be made may require more than one paragraph, but you should try to limit the development of the point to three paragraphs.
   - This is a dash-point paragraph, which is used to divide the thought in a numbered paragraph

     - You seldom break an idea down as far as dot-points but when you do it looks like this.

* * *

Besides these devices for dividing thoughts, you might also want to use stars (*) and paragraph points (l). Stars can be placed three in a row, in the center of the page, to indicate that a concluding comment to a long section is about to follow (see above). The paragraph point (l) can be used to set out lists when the number of items to be included is less than five (for example, for the section headings listed above), or to call attention to a single paragraph that contains a point to be emphasized.

- These paragraphs should be written in block form, and kept as short as possible.

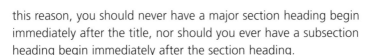

this reason, you should never have a major section heading begin immediately after the title, nor should you ever have a subsection heading begin immediately after the section heading.

6 *Don't overdo*. This is perhaps the most important rule of all. You want to use headings only if they are going to clarify your meaning – if they are going to make it easier for the reader to keep the subdivisions of your thought in his head. Often it is not necessary or useful to have any divisions below the major section headings.

If you formulate your headings properly, they will stand in the table of contents as a precis of your report – another extremely useful device for the reader in trying to come to terms with your thinking.

Underlined points

Another popular approach is literally to show the hierarchy of ideas by underlining the entire statement of the support points below the Key Line level (Exhibit 25). Lower level support points are also stated in their entirety, but distinguished by form and indentation.

The purpose of this format is to provide speed and ease in reading. The theory is that the reader should be able to speed through if he wishes, reading only the major underlined points, and in that way comprehend the entire message.

1 *You must be absolutely disciplined in applying question/answer logic*. Points below must directly answer the question raised by the point above, and no more. There is no room in this format for graceful liaisons of language or attempts at amplification. Such things destroy the clean, stark presentation of the logic. If you must amplify or give background, you will have to do so in the introductory or concluding paragraphs.

2 *You must be careful to word the points so that they state their message as sparsely as possible*. It destroys the ease with which the logic can be comprehended if the reader must wade through 30 words before he grasps the point. If you find yourself with more than a dozen words, or more than one subject and predicate, think again.

3 *You must be totally ruthless in limiting your points to the outline of your deductive or inductive argument*. Most people ignore this requirement and end up simply listing points, without regard to the niceties of either induction or deduction. You know that there are

never more than four points in a chained deductive argument, and never more than five in an inductive one. If you find yourself going beyond that, the likelihood is that you have overlooked an opportunity to group, and should rethink what you are saying.

Exhibit 25

REFLECT THE MAIN POINT IN THE TITLE

Write a paragraph or so for the situation xxx xxxxx xxxxxxxx xxx xxxxx xxxxxxxx xxx xxxxx xxxxxxxx xxxxx xxxx xxxxxxxx xxx xxxxx xxxxxxxx xxx xxxxx xxxxxxxx xxx xxxxx xxxx

Write a paragraph or so for the complication and the question. Sometimes the question is implied xxx xxxxx xxxxxxxx xxx xxxxx xxxxxxxx xxx xxxxx xxxxxxxx xxx xxxxx xxxxxxxx xxx xxxx xxxxxxxx xxx xxxxx xxxxxxxx xxx xxxxx xxxxxxxx xxx xxxxx xxxxxxxx xxx xxxx xxxxxxxx

State the main point. If the document is longer than seven paragraphs long, state the points on the key line:

- First Key Line point
- Second Key Line point
- Third Key Line point.

PUT A HEADING TO MATCH THE FIRST KEY LINE POINT

Write a short introduction leading up to and restating the main point. Again, if the section will be longer than seven paragraphs, state the points, centered, on the lines below, and then:

1. <u>NUMBER THE SUPPORT POINTS, IN UPPER CASE, AND UNDERLINE, AT THE MARGIN.</u>

    (1)<u>Indent, Number in Parentheses, the Points and Underline, in Upper and Lower Case, at the Next Level.</u>

    1. <u>If the Document is Very Long, Number Without Parentheses, Indent, and Underline, in Upper and Lower Case, the Points at the Next Level.</u>

        - Indent with a dot the points at the next level, capitalizing only the first word.
            - Indent with a dash the points at the next level, capitalizing only the first word. While this is lovely for the reader, it can be a bit difficult for the writer, because it imposes some strict rules on him.

Decimal numbering

Many companies, and most government institutions, like to use numbers rather than headings to emphasize the subdivisions of a document, and some go so far as to number every paragraph. This approach is claimed to have the advantage that any single topic or recommendation can be easily and precisely referred to.

However, frequent index numbers do tend to interrupt the reader's concentration on the content of the document, or on any section of it, as a whole.

If you decide that you prefer to have numbering because of its value as a quick guide, you would probably be wise to use it in conjunction with, rather than as a replacement for, headings. The headings have the value of enabling the reader to pick up the gist of the ideas quickly as he reads. And they are quite useful in refreshing his memory if he finds he has to go back to the document several days after his initial reading.

In addition, you will usually find that saying 'In Section 4.1 on manufacturing profits...' is clearer as a reference in jogging someone's comprehension and thinking than is saying only 'In Section 4.1...' In the former case, the person has the general idea in mind as he turns to the specific reference; in the latter, he must get to it before he can begin to think about it.

The excerpt shown in Exhibit 26, from the opening of Chapter 5 of Antony Jay's fine book, *Effective Presentation* (or *The New Oratory*, as it is known in the United States), illustrates the way you want your document to end up looking if you use the headings/ number form.

What numbering system should you use? This one is very common:

I. There is no other animal that will suffer to the death to aid its master as will a dog
   1. Other animals will run when danger nears
      a. The dog will remain
         i. Even though it might mean death.

This one is probably simpler to use:

1. There is no other animal that will suffer to the death to aid its master as will a dog
   1.1 Other animals will run when danger nears
      1.1.1 The dog will remain
         1.1.1.1 Even though it might mean death.

These examples show the relationships of the numbered levels to each other, rather than the actual form they should take. The form, as Exhibit 23 indicates, should reflect the actual divisions of thought in the piece of

Exhibit 26 Example of using headings and numbers

5. DELIVERY AND THE USE OF WORDS

Should the presenter have a written script, or just talk more or less spontaneously from a few notes? This is a constantly recurring question, and one to which more people come up with the wrong answer than any other.

To start with, let us agree that the best talker is the most natural. He is easy, fluent, friendly, amusing and free from the fetters that seem to bind others to small pieces of paper. He is just talking to us in the most natural way in the world: no script for him – how could there be? He is talking only to us and basing what he says on our reactions as he goes along. Such a talk cannot by definition be scripted.

5.1 THE PROBLEMS OF UNSCRIPTED PRESENTATION

For most of us, however, that sort of performance is an inspiration rather than a description. Our tongues are not so honeyed, and our words are less winged. And even for those who can on occasions touch those heights, there are three difficulties.

5.1.1. Visuals

A brilliant talker does not need visual aids to stop the audience from falling asleep, but the subject of a presentation very often demands them. And if you have them, it can be fatal to depart from the prepared order in which they are to appear. The slides and flip charts are in prearranged sequence, the operator has a fixed point at which to leave the slide machine and go outside to the film projector, and a brilliant extempore performance will mess the whole thing up.

5.1.2. Time

A presentation is almost always limited in time, and a certain amount has to be said in that time. Without fairly careful scripting, time is likely to be wildly overrun, or important points omitted.

5.1.3. The best way

If you accept that certain points have to be made in a certain time to a certain audience, the logic of optimization takes over. There is a best order in which to make the points. There is a best way of putting them to make them clear to the audience. There are best words and phrases to emphasize your arguments. Quite soon you discover that any genuinely spontaneous performance is not practicable, so it might as well all be scripted.

Most people get to this stage, and this is where it all goes wrong. They sit down at their desk, write out what they want to say, hand it to their secretary, and tell themselves that they have written their presentation. But they haven't. They have written a paper.

5.2 DON'T READ THEM A PAPER

I am not sure why it should be slightly offensive and insulting to have a document read to you, or obviously memorized and recited at you, in this sort of situation. Eminent professors read papers to learned societies, and no one complains: but in that case the audience are usually receiving (or hope they are receiving) a privileged preview of a new contribution to knowledge which will later be published...

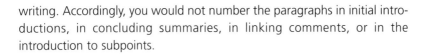

writing. Accordingly, you would not number the paragraphs in initial introductions, in concluding summaries, in linking comments, or in the
introduction to subpoints.

Indented display

Sometimes your document will be so short
that neither headings nor decimal numbering would be appropriate to highlight the divisions of your thinking. Nevertheless, you will still be dealing
with groupings of ideas, and you will want to highlight them in some way.

Groups of points supporting or explaining an overall idea are always
easier for the reader to absorb if they are set off so as to be easily distin-
guishable as a group. Consider, for example, the two versions of the
memorandum shown in Exhibit 27.

Exhibit 27-A

I have scheduled a Creative Thinking session with Frank
Griffith and the industrial engineers for the second week of
September, and for Al Beam and his staff for the third week
of September.

I think we need just a few slides to supplement the introduction,
which is attached with suggested slide concepts.

We also need slides of the Specific Examples of Positive
Reinforcement language. These slides would be used as a
wrap-up at the end of the presentation. This language should
also be in printed form to be used as a handout.

Slides showing the results of innovation we have had, such as
the slides that you made of the musical instruments, would
be quite valuable for the Frank Griffith meeting for the
second week, and they would be essential for the Al Beam
meeting set for the third week of September.

We have purchased the film 'Why Man Creates' to be used as
part of the introduction of the programme.

Slides are also needed for the section on Innovation
Environment Chart Traits.

The first version is perfectly clear as it stands; but the approach used in the second version makes the points literally 'jump out' at the reader.

Exhibit 27-B

I have scheduled a Creative Thinking session with Frank Griffith and the industrial engineers for the second week of September, and for Al Beam and his staff for the third week of September. For both these meetings I will need slides showing:

1 **The major points made in the introduction.** Suggested concepts are attached.

2 **Specific examples of positive reinforcement language.** These slides would be used as a wrap-up at the end of the presentation. This language should also be in printed form to be used as a handout.

3 **The results of innovation we have had**, such as the slides that you made of the musical instruments. These would be quite valuable for the Frank Griffith meeting, but essential for the Al Beam meeting.

4 **The steps needed to create an environment for innovation.** All of these devices serve as visual aids to the reader. They are meant to display to the reader's eye the logical relationships with which his mind is grappling, and in this way to help him comprehend them more quickly. Admittedly, they save only tiny amounts of the reader's time, but if he is a person who has scores of documents passing over his desk each day, the value of such small savings is considerable.

In general, the major rule to remember when you set your ideas off in this way is that you want to be sure to express them in the same grammatical form. Not only does this usually save words and make the ideas easier to grasp, but it also helps you to check whether you are saying clearly what you mean to say. Arranging the ideas in this way in Exhibit 27-B, for instance, shows up the fact that the author has not stated what kind of slides he wants for the section on Innovation Environment.

Whether the memorandum is long or short, the visual arrangement of groups of ideas to set off their similarity to each other as ideas will always make them easier to comprehend. As with headings, however, one set of indented groupings per memorandum is enough; otherwise the visual effect is lessened.

The
Pyramid
Principle

Introduction

to part II

As you try to apply The Pyramid Principle to a specific writing task, you should on most occasions, with a bit of practice, have little difficulty in creating an overall structure for your thinking. You can generally identify your Subject without much effort, determine the reader's Question, think through the Situation and the Complication, and proceed with a listing of your major points. With your title and major side headings decided, you can then settle to the serious business of putting it all into writing.

But no matter how carefully you have done your thinking in coming up with this initial structure, you are unlikely to produce a first draft that is perfectly logical and obeys all the rules. Points that seem to group logically in pyramid form often prove to have only a tenuous connection when clothed in prose. And watertight arguments have been known to spring gaping holes when you try to marshal valid support.

Unfortunately, you are unlikely to be able to see these flaws without making a special effort to do so. Once you put ideas in writing, they take on an incredible beauty in the author's eyes. They seem to glow with a fine patina that you will be quite reluctant to disturb.

The most efficient way to overcome this psychological impediment is to have a checklist of rules you apply to every grouping in the structure, so that you are forced to look at it critically. In this way your parental pride is backed into abeyance, and you can be objective about what you see. (This approach applies equally effectively, of course, to reading someone else's draft.)

There are essentially four sets of such rules available to help you focus your critical faculties:

1 You can question the general *order* of the ideas in a grouping.
2 You can question their particular *source* in your problem-solving process.
3 You can question your *summary statement* about them.
4 You can question the *prose* in which you express them.

The following chapters explain the theory and practice behind each of these techniques. In reading this material, it may strike you that some parts are both more technical and more abstract than you are used to from the earlier chapters. Alas, there seems to be no other way to explain the concepts clearly than to outline the theory behind them first. However, proper application of the concepts is so essential to clear writing that I'm sure you will find the extra effort required to understand the theory well worthwhile.

Questioning the order of a grouping

You know that ideas in any grouping must be placed in logical order. In deductive groupings, of course, that is no problem, since logical order is the order imposed by the structure of the argument. In inductive groupings, however, you have a choice of how to order. Thus, you need to know how to make the choice, and how to judge that you have made the right choice.

To this end you must understand that ideas grouped together in writing are never brought there by chance. They are always picked out of your mind because it sees them as having a logical relationship. For example:

- Three steps to solve a problem.
- Three key factors for success in an industry.
- Three problems in a company.

To see such relationships, the mind must have performed a logical analysis. In that case, the order you choose should reflect the analytical activity that your mind performed to create the grouping. The mind can perform only three analytical activities of this nature (Exhibit 28).

1 *It can determine the causes of an effect*. Whenever you make statements in writing that tell the reader to do something – fire the sales manager, say, or delegate profit responsibility to the regions – you do so because you believe the action will have a particular effect. You have determined in advance the effect you want to achieve, and then identified the action necessary to achieve it.

   When several actions are together required to achieve the effect (e.g., three steps to solve a problem), they become a process or a system – the set of causes that in concert create the effect. The steps required to complete the process or implement the system can only be carried out one at a time, over time. Thus, a grouping of steps that represents a process or system always goes in *time order*.

Exhibit 28 The source of the grouping   ...dictates its order

1. *It can determine the causes of an effect*   *Time order*

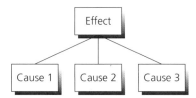

2. *It can divide a whole into its parts*   *Structual order*

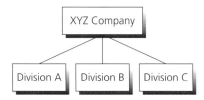

3. *It can classify like things*   *Ranking order*

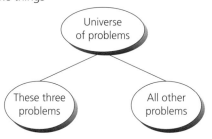

2 *It can divide a whole into its parts.* You are familiar with this technique in creating organization charts or picturing the structure of an industry. If you are going to determine the 'key factors for success in an industry,' for example, you must first visualize the structure of that industry. Having done so, you determine what must be done well to succeed in each part of it. The resulting grouping of three or four key factors would then logically be ordered to match the order of the parts shown in the structure you visualized. This is *structural order*.

3 *It can classify like things together.* Whenever you say that a company 'has three problems,' you are not speaking literal truth. The company has many problems – some total universe of problems – of which you have classified three as being noteworthy in some way compared to the others. You are saying that each possesses a characteristic by which you are able to identify it as a particular kind of problem – say because each one is the result of a refusal to delegate authority.

All three problems are the same in that each possesses this characteristic, but they are all different in that each possesses it to a different degree. (If they possessed it to the same degree, you could not distinguish between them on this basis.) Because they are different, therefore, you rank them in the order in which they possess to the greatest degree whatever characteristic made you identify them as problems in the first place. This is called *ranking order*.

These orders can be applied singly or in combination, but one of them must always be present in a grouping. Let me tell you more about each of them and how you can use them to check your thinking.

Time order

Time order is the simplest order of all to understand, and the most pervasive in business writing. What you are doing in a time-ordered grouping is spelling out the steps a person must take to achieve a particular effect, in the order in which he must take them.

Although it seems a simple discipline to impose, it is extraordinary how frequently people fail to impose it. Consequently, the most common logical flaw you are likely to find in a first draft is improper time groupings. The trick in sorting them out is to visualize yourself taking the actions in each case.

Ask yourself, 'What would I do first if I were doing this? What second? etc.' Answering the question can help you to uncover instances where your thinking has been incomplete, your logic confused, or your grouping false.

Incomplete thinking

Try the questioning of the order on this example:

Strategic planning involves the recognition of a timing cycle.
Perception of need.
Development of strategy for creating responsive product/service.
Implementation.
Market acceptance and high growth.
Slower growth, the onset of maturity.
High cash generation.
Decline/decay.

Were you reviewing this for sense, you would be looking to see that they are indeed all the steps in the cycle and that they are in the right order. Put yourself in the doer's place. First you would perceive the need, then you would develop a strategy, then implement the strategy, then. . . Oops, here is a problem.

What the author appears to have done is to group three actions the company takes and four things that result. If you look at the results for a moment, you can see that he is reflecting the normal product life-cycle curve in which you get:

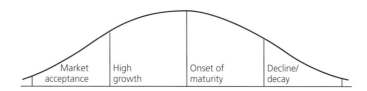

Thus, he must mean his fourth step to be something like 'Track the market's reaction,' with these points as the path of that reaction. We do have one point left over: high cash generation. This, however, is normally a characteristic of the onset-of-maturity phase, so does not belong in the list at all.

Confused logic

That was a relatively simple example of incomplete thinking. But the technique is equally useful when the logic is badly confused, as in this example:

> However, business definition. . .
>> Relies heavily on creative processes.
>>> Demand segmentation.
>>> Supply segmentation.
>> Changes over time.
>>> Early vs. late stages of life cycle.
>>> Competitive dynamics.
>> Not necessarily unique in a given industry.
>>> Influenced by marketer's own strength vs. competition.

Whatever can he mean? Is it time order that he is talking about in carrying out the act of business definition: first you be creative, then you change, then. . . No, that doesn't make sense. What are the actions implied here? Segmentation, review for changes, assessment of competitive strengths. Now can you see an order?

> Business definition requires careful analysis:
>> In defining market segments.
>> In assessing your competitive position in each segment.
>> In tracking changes in position over time.

False grouping

You can see the power of the technique in identifying improper order because of confused logic. It also lets you identify when you have brought ideas together that don't belong in the grouping, as here:

> The traditional focus of investment evaluation is to compare future returns and probable costs.
>> It is often technically unsound.
>> It rests on simplistic concepts.
>> It results in misleading prescriptions.

Are these ideas in order of importance? In time order? In structural order? Or in none of the above? If you look critically you can see that the third idea is the effect of the other two. Thus, he seems to be saying:

> Evaluating investments by comparing future returns to probable costs results in misleading prescriptions.
>> The concept itself is simplistic.
>> Its application is often technically unsound.

The order is time order, in the sense that you have to have the concept before you can apply it badly. But do you need more than a bad concept and bad application of it for misleading prescriptions to result? Is the first one alone enough? I don't know the answer. What I am trying to demonstrate here is that once you impose a logical order on the ideas, you are then in a position to check that the thinking is complete. You cannot do so while the concept itself is unclear.

Sometimes you will find that time order is imposed on an existing structure, so that the structure dictates the number and sequence of steps. To that end let's look at structural order.

Structural order

First, what exactly is structural order? It is the order that reflects what you see once you have visualized something – either by diagram or map, by drawing or photograph. The 'something' you visualize can be real or conceptual, an object or a process. It must, however, have been properly divided to show its parts.

Creating a structure

When you divide a whole into its parts – whether it be a physical whole or a conceptual one – you must make sure that the pieces you produce are:

- *Mutually exclusive* of each other.
- *Collectively exhaustive* in terms of the whole.

I abbreviate this mouthful to MECE, but it is a concept you no doubt apply automatically every time you create an organization chart (Exhibit 29). Mutually exclusive means that what goes on in the Tire Division is not duplicated in Housewares, and what goes on in Sports Equipment is distinct from both. In other words, no overlaps. Collectively exhaustive means that what goes on in all three divisions is everything that goes on in the Akron Tire and Rubber Company. In other words, nothing left out.

If you apply these rules when you divide, you can be sure that the structure you create shows all the pieces that must be described if you are to explain it to someone else. Structural order at its simplest, then, means that you will describe the pieces of the structure as they appear on the diagram.

But how do you know what order to put them in on the diagram? This question most frequently arises when people draw organization charts. The order you put the boxes in on an organization chart will reflect the principle of division you employed to create them.

Exhibit 29 A typical organization chart

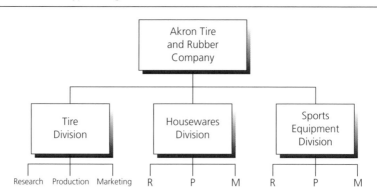

There are basically three ways to divide the activities of an organization – by the activities themselves (e.g., research, marketing, production), by the location in which the activities take place (e.g., Eastern Region, Midwest, West), or by sets of activities directed to a particular product, market, or customer (e.g., Tires, Housewares, Sports Equipment).

- If you divide to emphasize the activities, they reflect a process, and thus go in time order.
- If you divide to emphasize location, they go in structural order, reflecting the realities of geography.
- If you divide to emphasize activities relating to a single product/market, you have classified, and thus the ideas go in ranking order, by whatever measure you decide is relevant for ranking (e.g., sales, investment).

Thus, suppose you had created this set of departments in reorganizing a city government:

1 Housing
2 Transportation
3 Education
4 Recreation
5 Personal health
6 Environmental health

These are the activities for which you think the city is responsible, and the order in which you put them reflects the order in which the city government would have to be concerned about its populace if it were starting the city from scratch. Forcing yourself to see an order, particularly if you are creating something new like an organization, permits you to check that you have been collectively exhaustive for your purposes.

In dividing things other than organizations, however, your purpose is generally to analyze how those things function. You are therefore dividing by functioning part, and you show the parts in the order in which they would be expected to perform that function. Thus, if you were discussing a radar set, you would order its parts to reflect the order of their functioning:

1 Modulator
2 Radio-frequency oscillator
3 Antenna with suitable scanning mechanism
4 Receiver
5 Indicator

The modulator takes in power that the oscillator then gives out. The antenna concentrates that power into a beam, the receiver takes in signals passed back from the beam's scanner, and the indicator in turn presents the data.

Describing a structure

Once the structure is set up, one way to describe it is to follow it from the top down and from left to right, describing each part in the order in which it appears. This is the form you would follow if you were giving a technical description of the radar set described above, or any other technical description of a piece of machinery.

However, you can also impose a process order on your description. To illustrate, on page 99 is a map of the Sinai Desert. The passage following describes its structure.

The 'contexts' in which one can view the map are listed in the order in which the eye would comprehend them as it began to look at the map. First, it would fasten on the wedge, because it's so obvious. Then it would see the split from Egypt, then the southern part of Israel, then the top of Saudi Arabia. Finally, it would travel back from east to west. Thus, the author has visualized the process a reader would follow in examining the map, and reflected that order in his description.

Visualizing a process in relationship to a structure is a common device, particularly if you are writing to recommend changes to an existing structure. Suppose, for example, you had the structure of a city government shown at the top of Exhibit 31, and you were recommending replacing it with that shown at the bottom.

You would be recommending four changes to get from the first structure to the second. In what order should you state them? They are all equally important, so you cannot put them in order of importance. They must, in theory, all be done at the same time, so that kind of time order is not appropriate.

Exhibit 30 Map of the Sinai Desert

(From *The New Yorker*, June 4, 1979, 'Sinai: The Great and Terrible Wilderness' by Burton Bernstein.)

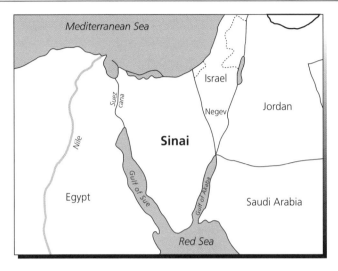

On any map of the Middle East, the Sinai Peninsula sits dead center, an almost perfect inverted isosceles triangle, a sharp wedge that seems to cleave Africa from Arab Asia. Depending on one's political persuasion, it can be seen in several other contexts: as an eastern arm of Egypt, holy Egyptian soil, severed from its motherland only a little more than a century ago by the Suez Canal; as a natural and logical southern extension of Israel, a massive broadening of the Negev Desert; as a northern adjunct of Saudi Arabia, separated from that immensity by the narrow Gulf of Akaba; or, simply, as an ancient land bridge connecting East and West, a handy route for caravans and invading armies.

The order that makes most sense in a case like this is the order in which you would draw the elements on a blank sheet of paper if you were presenting them to the reader one at a time. Thus, my first step would be to group the many departments into the six shown. The second step would be to put the Policy and Finance Committee in charge of the whole. The third step would be to create the two groups to support the Committee, and the final one would be to create the administrative team needed to manage the paperwork.

Imposing a structure

You can also use the concept of structural order to help you sort out faulty logic in a grouping. Suppose you had this set of steps presented to you for your approval:

Exhibit 31 Structures of a City Government

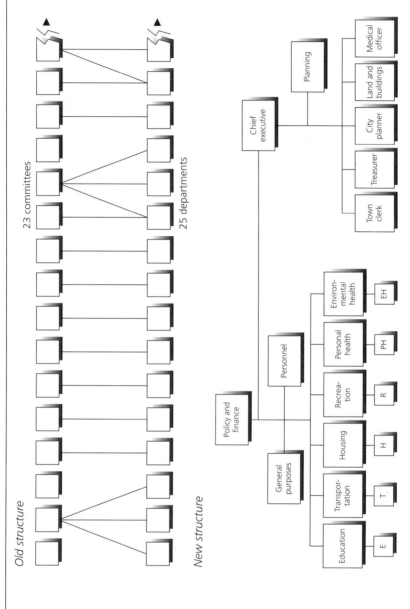

Old structure

23 committees

25 departments

New structure

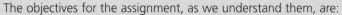

The objectives for the assignment, as we understand them, are:

1 To review and analyze field operations in maintenance and construction areas.
2 To determine if adequate organizational and managerial flexibility exists to allow field engineers to properly respond to day-to-day operating problems and demands from the public.
3 To review and analyze the areas of preliminary engineering, road and bridge design, environmental process, right-of-way acquisition and traffic management.
4 To review and analyze the organization structure of the Department.
5 To identify the strengths and weaknesses within each study area.

Why this order? Where did these ideas come from? First of all, you can see that point 5 does not go with the others because it refers to them all, so we can eliminate that. Then let's see what subjects he's talking about in the others:

1 Maintenance, construction
2 Day-to-day operations
3 Preliminary engineering, road bridge and bridge design
  Environmental process, right-of-way acquisition,
  traffic management
4 Organization structure.

If we attempt to see them in terms of a process concerned with road-building, etc., you would assume the steps involved would be these:

1 Design
2 Construct
3 Operate
4 Maintain

In that case, perhaps the author meant to say that the objective for the assignment would be to determine whether the Department is properly organized and managed to carry out its activities, of which there are four.

Ranking order

Finally, we come to ranking order, or order of importance. This is the order you impose on a grouping when it brings together a set of things you have classified as being alike because they possess a characteristic in common – e.g., three problems, four reasons, five variables.

Creating proper class groupings

In classifying, when you say, 'The company has three problems,' your mind automatically separates these three problems from all other possible problems the company has or could have, creating a bifurcate structure like that shown in Exhibit 32. The two classes formed are by definition collectively exhaustive, and are of course meant to be mutually exclusive.

You prove they are mutually exclusive by defining quite specifically what characteristic they have in common, and then searching your knowledge to make sure you have included in your grouping all known items with this same characteristic. Then you place them in the order of the degree to which each possesses the characteristic by which you classified it – presenting the strongest one first.

(Many people ask me whether, having determined the relative weight of the points, you always have to put the strongest one first. They point out that it would be more dramatic to put the weakest one first and work up to the strongest one. It would indeed be more dramatic, but would it be clearer? I think not, and so I prefer strongest-to-weakest. However, this is a question of style, predicated on appeal to emotions, and in some cases you may quite legitimately decide to reverse the order for greater emotional impact.)

Exhibit 32 Classification limits your thinking to a narrow universe*

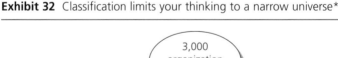

*...have a set of things in common you can rank

Were the process described above all there is to classifying ideas, there would be very little to say about problems in ordering them. However, classifying is a ubiquitous human habit. People classify everything they see as soon as they see it, simply by naming what it is. Unfortunately, when they come to ideas they do not limit themselves only to creating classes of points that are alike by virtue of their possessing a characteristic in common. They also consider ideas to be alike, and therefore classifiable, if they were derived from the same process or drawn from the same *structure*.

This is a perfectly legitimate thing to do in writing, provided that you are clear about the source of your grouping and reflect accordingly the order it imposes. But more often than not, the great pleasure authors feel in having thought up three or four points to include in a grouping prevents them from questioning the logic of its origin.

Let me give you an example of perfectly acceptable, but indiscriminate classifying, and then show you how to use this knowledge to discover flaws in what seem like proper class groupings.

Several years ago Bankers Trust Company reprinted a 1921 piece by James Harvey Robinson called *The Mind in the Making*. In it Robinson said:

'We do not think enough about thinking, and much of our confusion is the result of current illusions in regard to it. Let us forget for the moment any impressions we may have derived from the philosophers, and see what seems to happen in ourselves.'

He then proceeded to classify the various kinds of thinking as shown in Exhibit 33. You see there four class groupings. Only the first and third of these appear to reflect the act of grouping by common characteristic. The second and fourth present a process, answering the question 'How?' Looking at the first grouping for a moment, the technique I use to determine its validity is to question its origin:

1 What does he label the points as?
   Things that determine the course of the reverie.
2 Can I find anything more specifically the same about them?
   They are all emotional reactions we have to the world.
3 Can I justify their order on that basis?
   Most commonly felt reaction first.
4 Are there any missing?
   Probably not.

Exhibit 33 The Classes of Thinking

You may, of course, disagree with this assessment, and you may be right. The point is that to check the thinking for completeness, you must be able to identify its source and make sure you have included all that the source produces. In this case I can't think of any other emotional reactions that people have to the world around them, but you may be able to do so. If you can, then you have enlarged on his thinking; if you can't, then you must concede that his reasoning makes sense.

Looking in the same way at the third grouping (Rationalizing our beliefs and opinions), the first breakdown shows the MECE ways in which we acquire beliefs and opinions. Moving down a level on the first one:

1 What does he label the points as?
   Cherished convictions about which we feel certain.
2 Can I find anything more specifically the same about them?
   They all reflect the influence of early teaching.
3 Can I justify their order on that basis?
   Order in which the teaching would be absorbed? I don't
   think so.
4 Are there any missing?
   Rather it would seem there are too many, specifically the
   beliefs about property and business.

What difference does it make, you may ask, whether the grouping is over-complete or incomplete? It will affect the way in which the inference you draw from the groupings is accepted as true by the reader. If overcomplete, your statement will not apply equally to the points below. If incomplete, someone else adding members to it could draw a different inference.

In this case, for example, the author's summary statement was:

- We like to continue to believe what we have been accustomed to accept as true, and the resentment aroused when doubt is cast upon any of our assumptions leads us to seek every manner of excuse for clinging to them.

That may be true of religion, the family, our country, and the state. I find it difficult, however, to envision people jumping to defend the concept of property or ideas about business with quite the same emotional intensity.

By contrast, the summary to the first grouping said this:

- A great part of our spontaneous thinking is far too intimate, personal, ignoble, or trivial to permit us to reveal more than a small part of it.

It appears to apply equally to all three points and we cannot think of others to add to the grouping.

To repeat, my purpose here is to show you that groupings are not just drawn out of the air, but reflect an analytical assessment that implies a strict order. You want deliberately to look for this order in every class grouping so that you can be certain you are saying what you mean.

Identifying improper class groupings

To show you the difference it can make to your thinking, let's look at some examples. Suppose you came across this:

> The traditional financial focus of investment evaluation results in misleading prescriptions for corporate behavior. . .
>> Corporations should invest in all opportunities where probable returns exceed the cost of capital.
>> Better quantification of future uncertainty and risk is the key to more effective resource allocation.
>> Planning and capital budgeting are two separate processes; capital budgeting is a financial activity.
>> Top management's role is to challenge the numbers rather than the underlying thinking.

Now apparently these are the four misleading prescriptions that result from the traditional financial focus. More specifically, they are commonly believed 'rules of thumb' in corporations. But are they? If you reword them as results, they say, to abbreviate them:

> Encourages corporations to invest.
> Emphasizes quantification of uncertainty.
> Separates planning and capital budgeting.
> Leads top management to focus on the numbers.

All but the third can now be seen as part of a process of decision making, which would dictate a different order, which in turn would lead to a clearer point at the top:

> The traditional financial focus of investment evaluation can result in poor resource allocation decisions:
>> Emphasizes quantification of future uncertainty and risk as the key to choosing among projects.
>> Leads top management to focus on the numbers rather than the underlying thinking.
>> Encourages investment in all opportunities where probable returns exceed the cost of capital, ignoring other considerations.

That one was easy to sort out because the kind of idea you were dealing with was easy to identify simply by reading it. Very often, however, you will find yourself with several kinds of ideas whose class membership is not that easy to see at first reading.

> Problems with sales and inventory systems reports:
> 1 Report frequency is inappropriate.
> 2 Inventory data is unreliable.
> 3 Inventory data is too late.
> 4 Inventory data cannot be matched to sales data.
> 5 People want reports with better formats.
> 6 People want elimination of meaningless data.
> 7 People want exception highlighting.
> 8 People want to do fewer calculations manually.

The trick is to go through and sort them into rough categories, as a prelude to looking more critically later. You get the categories by defining the *kind of problem* they are discussing:

> **Timing**
> 1 Report frequency is inappropriate
> 3 Inventory data are too late
>
> **Data**
> 2 Inventory data is unreliable
> 4 Inventory data cannot be matched to sales data
> 6 People want elimination of meaningless data
>
> **Format**
> 5 People want better report formats
> 7 People want exception highlighting
> 8 People want to do fewer calculations manually.

You have a double ordering task here. First, in what order do you put timing, data, and format? That depends on the process you think they reflect. Here we have two possibilities: we could be talking about the process of preparing the reports, or we could be talking about the process of reading the reports.

If you are talking about preparing the reports, you would complain first about the data, then about the format, then about the timing, because that is the order in which the preparer would deal with them. On the other hand, if you are talking about reading the reports, you would complain first about the timing, then about the format, then about the data, for the same reason.

How about ordering the ideas in each grouping? Under Timing, points 1 and 3 should probably be reversed, as you worry about lateness before you worry about frequency. Under Data, I should think you would complain first that a good deal of the data are meaningless, what is not meaningless is unreliable, and what is reliable can't be matched. Process order again. Under Format, points 7 and 8 would be subsets of point 5, with the 'fewer calculations' probably coming before the 'highlighting.'

A great value of the exercise has been to show that in some areas the thinking is incomplete, so that the author can review his analysis. Here's another example:

> The causes of New York's decline are many and complex. Among them are:
> 1 Wage rates higher than those that prevail elsewhere in the country.
> 2 High energy, rent and land costs.
> 3 Traffic congestion that forces up transportation costs.
> 4 A lack of modern factory space.
> 5 High taxes.
> 6 Technological change.
> 7 The competition of new centers of economic concentration in the Southwest and the West.
> 8 The refocusing of American economic and social life in the suburbs.

This is a good example of 'truism' in argument. What in effect the author is saying is:

> - Everybody knows that there are lots of reasons for New York's decline.
> - Here are some of them.
> - Therefore. . . (?) on to the next subject.

The problem with such 'for instancing' is that it cannot lead you logically to consider what you do about the problems. As a partial list it communicates nothing, because you cannot draw a clear inference from it.

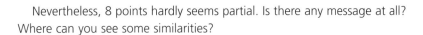

Nevertheless, 8 points hardly seems partial. Is there any message at all? Where can you see some similarities?

Costs
1   High wage rates.
2   High energy, rent, land.
3   High transportation.
5   High taxes.

Unsuitability of area
4   Lack of modern factory space to modernize into.
6   Technological change (leading to need to modernize).
8   Business associates moved to suburbs.

Alternative choice
7   New centers in the Southwest and West.

Perhaps he means to be saying this:

The causes of New York's decline reflect in part the growth of new business centers:
It has always been a high-cost city in which to do business.
More attractive areas are springing up in the Southwest and West
Thus, when companies face the need to move, they choose to move south.

This may not be at all what the author meant to say, but it is what an interested reader might glean from his listing. By pointing out what it does seem to be saying, you give the author the opportunity to rewrite it, to say more clearly what he does mean.

I want to give you just one more example. It is a very difficult one, in that it is almost a free association of points. However, given our technique it is relatively easy to work out. And it does demonstrate that the author had a structure in his head before he began to write. He simply reflected his comprehension of it badly.

It is written by someone in a soft-drinks manufacturing company that had decided to put its product into plastic rather than glass bottles. It could buy the plastic bottles on the outside, or it could create its own plastic bottle manufacturing capability.

There are a number of internal/external risks and constraints that preclude an investment in any plastic bottle venture:

1 Technical risk – undeveloped design problems.
2 Environmental risk – legislated nonreturnable ban.
3 Premium risk – consumer rejection of a premium package during an inflationary period.
4 Nonexclusivity: (a) outside sales diminish marketing impact, (b) sales to others may be difficult with our ownership.
5 Capital intensiveness – the project has an extremely long payback period.
6 Negative EPS impact (accentuated by leveraging).
7 Near-term R&D expense.
8 Corporate cash flow problems – funds needed for expansion of existing business.
9 Price slashing by glass manufacturers and/or lower than projected glass inflation rate vis-à-vis plastic.
10 Other plastic manufacturers may effect dramatic price cuts upon entry due to lower return on investment goals (many are in 7–10% range).
11 Entry in the container industry which is typified by lower margins and in which the key is to be the lowest cost producer. Implicit in the entry is the probable downward reassessment of our P/E.

This looks like a terrible mess, but the sorting process for fixing it would be the same as in other cases. First, go down the list and see why he is complaining about each point. Why is each one considered to be a bad thing? This will allow you to see some patterns.

1 High cost
2 Prevented by law from doing
3 Force lower sales or lower price
4 Low sales
5 High investment, low ROI
6 Lower EPS
7 High cost
8 Must borrow
9 Force lower price
10 Force lower price
11 Low margins, lower P/E.

Whenever business people talk about things like costs, sales, prices, investment, and ROI, they are implying their knowledge of the relationships
between these things as displayed on a standard ROI tree. If you impose
the relevant points on such a tree, it is relatively easy to see what his message is:

The points about Earnings per Share and Price/Earnings Ratio suggest
another tree:

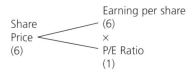

We are then left with two points: No. 8, we must borrow, and No. 2, there
is a risk that we won't be able to sell because of a ban on nonreturnable
bottles. The borrowing point can be fitted into the tree if I add another
layer below profits to make room for taxes and interest. I've left this out to
make the technique easier to comprehend.

If we try to put it all together, he appears to be saying:

> We should think carefully before going into the plastic bottle
> business:
>   If there is a nonreturnable ban, we may be precluded from doing so.
>   Even if there is no ban, it would dilute our profitability.
>   Short term, lower EPS.
>   Long term, lower ROI.

Now that you see what the message is, you can scrutinize the individual
points to make sure they are properly supported. I would guess they are
not, only because I know that this particular company did go into the plastic bottle business and has made an immense success of it. What was left
out of the author's thinking, apparently, was an assessment of the effect
of plastic containers on the sales of the product.

The point I wish to reiterate is that you cannot tell that nonsense is being written unless you first impose a structure on it. It is the imposition of the structure that permits you to see flaws and omissions.

To summarize, I have tried to demonstrate with all these examples that checking order is a key means of checking the validity of a grouping. With any grouping of inductive ideas that you are reviewing for sense, always begin by running your eye quickly down the list. Are they indeed all from the same source: a process, a structure, a class? Are they all in logical order: time order if the source is a process, structural order if the source is a structure, ranking order if the source is a class.

Once you know the grouping is valid, you are in a position to draw a logical inference from it, as explained in Chapter 9.

Questioning the problem-solving process

8

As you saw in Chapter 7, one of the reasons people group together ideas in writing that do not have a clear logical relationship is that they have unconsciously drawn them haphazardly from a preconceived structure. By forcing themselves actually to visualize the structure, they can match their points to it. Thus, they can check not only that the points are in the right order, but also that all those that should be included are included.

In the particular example I gave, the structure was that of a Department responsible for building and maintaining a state highway system. Once you saw the match between its activities and the ideas in the grouping, the proper order became obvious.

The document from which the grouping was taken came from a consulting firm, and is known as a Letter of Proposal. Such letters spell out for a prospective client what his problem is and how the consulting firm proposes to go about solving it. If the proposal is accepted, the consulting firm will then carry out the analyses required to solve the problem and write a report embodying its findings, conclusions, and recommendations.

Coming up with those findings, conclusions, and recommendations requires the creation and use of a number of analytical structures. These structures, in turn, must be referred to in checking the order and completeness of the ideas generated by them.

Those of you who write documents that detail the results of problem solving, whether in consulting or in business, may find it useful to review the general problem-solving process and some of the analytical structures associated with it, as a basis for looking critically at what is said.

The problem-solving process

Ideally, problem solving begins with problem setting – i.e., identifying precisely what you mean by 'the problem' and how you will know when you have achieved a solution. When you identify a problem, essentially what you do is recognize that a particular situation yields a specific result.

The problem is either that you do not like the result (e.g., Sales are down 10 percent), or that you cannot explain the result (e.g., What determines what we think? Is it the structure of the brain? Is it our genetic makeup?) Changing the result in the first instance calls for the application of routine problem-solving skills. Finding the explanation in the second demands the somewhat more creative hypothesizing of scientists and inventors.

I am talking here about routine problem solving. (See the Appendix for a discussion of creative problem solving.) This process has been described in a number of different, sometimes conflicting, ways. The simplest, most practical description I have seen was set out by my friend B. Robert Holland in his manual, *Sequential Analysis*, published by McKinsey & Company in 1972. According to Holland, the process consists of answering a series of questions in logical sequence:

1 What is the problem?
2 Where does it lie?
3 Why does it exist?
4 What could we do about it?
5 What should we do about it?

The answer to each question must be structured visually before you can be said fully to understand what you have found. Let me take you through the sequence using a simple example, and then show you how creating the structures required at each stage can aid you in writing clearly about your results.

In doing so, let me point out that I recognize that you may in fact not go about problem solving in this clean, compelling manner. The problem situation you face can be very murky, and information can come at you in a random way, in a variety of misleading or overwhelming forms. And you always have the personalities of the people with whom you are working to consider. What I am advocating, however, is that when you sit down to put your thoughts in order prior to writing, you try to force an analytical structure on your findings and conclusions.

The example I will use is this: Suppose that you are a cigarette manufacturer and you discover that the productivity of the machines in Department A is lower than the productivity of the machines in all your other departments – i.e., Department A turns out fewer cigarettes per machine than the others.

What is the problem?

The problem is that you do not like the result. But that is not a complete definition of the problem. To what precisely do you object? How will you know when the problem is solved? In effect, what question do you want your analysis to answer?

What you want to do here is to try to create a clear image of exactly what you mean. You may have to gather some data in order to answer the question, but it should be easily available. For example, this particular company measured its machines in terms of productive hours per day, and the figures were available for each machine. The useful image, then, would probably be some visualization between the good performers and the poor ones.

Now you can say to yourself, 'We're losing 2 hours of productivity a day. What I want to know is what is causing those lost hours? Or more specifically, how do I eliminate the causes of lost hours?'

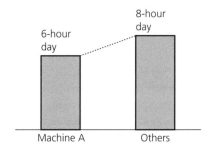

Where does the problem lie?

Next you gather the data that will allow you to picture the situation within which the problem occurs – i.e., the set of activities that produce lost hours. This will enable you to isolate all the possible ways in which lost hours of production could be caused.

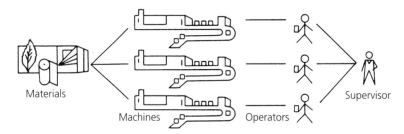

In this case five possible things could be going wrong: no materials at the machines, broken machines, no operator, poor operator, or poor supervisor. These are the possibilities that you must investigate.

In creating a useful structure of the situation, you are trying to show how the elements in the situation relate functionally and interact as a system to accomplish a specific purpose. Sometimes these relationships are not at all obvious, so that to diagram them you must first do a good deal of digging. Keep digging until (1) you are sure you have identified all the parts in the system, (2) you can arrange them in sequential order, and (3) you can clearly show inputs and outputs.

Why does the problem exist?

The overall structure of the situation will indicate a number of directions in which your analysis can proceed. In our cigarette example we know we can gather facts that let us judge whether the machines were without raw material, or without maintenance, etc. – a relatively simple exercise.

In more complex situations, however, you will have to probe more deeply into both the things and the processes that make up the structure. You will be trying to make clear the components of each, their importance to each other, and how they change over time. (A number of analytical structures have been developed that permit you to initiate this probing and display its results so that they can be thought about productively. I will talk about several of the most useful of these in the next section.)

Clearly, in these more complex situations you will also have to be selective. Not all possibilities are likely to prove equally important in solving the problem. Consequently, you will have to make a judgment early on about which areas deserve the greatest concentration of effort. Such judgments can only be based on experience in the industry or in solving similar problems, and are thus generally made by senior members of the consulting staff.

What could we do about it?

Once the situation has been visualized and analyzed, so that you know why the problem exists, you have a good idea of what needs to be changed. However, there may appear to be alternative ways to change, each of which derives logically from the structure of the activity under study. They must now be tested to determine which way most effectively creates the desired result.

In our cigarette company example, the problem turned out to be that the operators were not 'tuning up' their machines properly, which in turn was the result of inadequate training by their superiors. How could one go about improving the supervision, then?

You could make the job of training new operators a specific objective in judging the supervisor's performance, you could transfer a supervisor from a more productive department to this one, or you could increase the number of supervisors. Which course of action makes most sense depends on its feasibility and on its likelihood of success (on its benefits and risks, if you like), which must be thoroughly assessed before you choose.

What should we do about it?

In making the decision to choose one alternative over the next, you must be able to visualize the new situation with the change implemented. Creating this picture should suggest to you the additional changes that must be made to accommodate it, and once again highlight the points that need analysis and verification before you make a final recommendation.

With the numerical consequences clear, you next want to explore the risks involved in achieving them. Risks in this context would generally be of three kinds: you will have made a mistake in your assumptions, you might not achieve your objective, or you may inspire retaliation of some kind. Should it look as though the choice is very risky for any one of these reasons, you would want to stop considering it as an alternative.

What this section has been saying is that before you can legitimately advise someone on how to change an undesirable result, you must have defined clearly five things: (1) the gap between where he is and where he wants to be, (2) the structure of the situation that gave rise to the gap, (3) the structure of its underlying processes, (4) the alternative ways the structure could be changed, and (5) the changes required to accommodate the alternative you choose.

You can see that completion of Step 1 tells you not only how to direct your analysis of the problem, but also how to write your introduction. It identifies the question your report must be structured to answer. Steps 2 and 3 identify the major analyses that must be completed before you can formulate recommendations to answer the question.

Thus, in looking critically at the draft of a report, you will want to make sure first that the introduction reflects a clear definition of the problem, and then that the findings and conclusions derive from appropriate analytical structures. Chances are that you will find glaring omissions in both cases.

Defining the problem
As I noted earlier, the likelihood is that you will not have done your problem solving in quite the neat and tidy way described, particularly where you face very complex problem situations. If you feel you have solved the problem, however, you will no doubt

have generated sufficient data to be able to re-create the structures used to define the problem, showing:

- Where you are now.
- Where you want to be.
- The difference between the two.

The ease with which re-creating these structures can help you decide what to say in your introduction and how to set up your pyramid may amaze you. To demonstrate that ease, let's look at the introduction shown in Exhibit 34, *DDT: A System for Document Digitalization and Teletransmission*.

The DDT system

Here we have an extremely densely written text. What it says is approximately as follows:

> S = We did a study in 1989 telling how documents could be stored and transmitted by computer. Research Institute also did a study on the problems of transmitting documents on Euronet/DIANE.
>
> C = You recommended more technical studies. We have been looking at the technological, economic and managerial issues of converting documents to digital form and delivering them by teletransmission. This is because technology is rapidly developing that could permit electronic document delivery.
>
> Q =
>
> A = It is technically possible to do at reasonable cost on a European scale.
> - We conceived a system to build on DIANE called DDT
> - Market forces will not bring such a system about, it demands a demonstration project.
> - DDT must be an open system, based on international standards.
> - Further technical studies are needed.
> - Important nontechnical issues must be resolved.

Ignoring the sheer ugliness of the title, the text permits very little sense of the problem it was dealing with to shine through. What in fact is the problem, and what is the question concerning it? 'Looking at the technological, economic and managerial issues of converting documents to digital form and delivering them by teletransmission' is not very specific. To make it more specific, you must ask yourself, what do they have now and how do they want to change it?

What they have now, apparently, if you read the text closely, is a situation in which someone scans a televised listing to locate a document, and telephones a library requesting it. The library locates the document, has it copied, and mails the copy to the requester. Total elapsed time, 7 to 10 days.

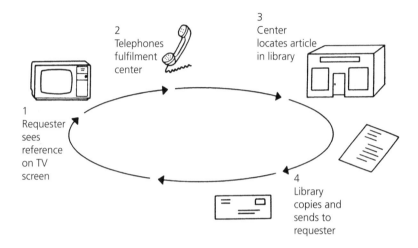

What they would like instead is a system in which TV listing, telephones for the document, and receives it back on his screen within an hour.

Given this understanding of the problem, and a clear statement of how you will know when you have solved it, you can easily identify the question the analysis is meant to solve: Can we reduce the retrieval time from 10 days to 1 hour by transmitting the document electronically?

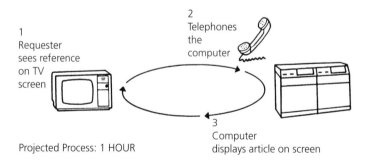

A glance at the initial picture lets you see what would have to change structurally to permit this to happen:

Exhibit 34 DDT: a system for documentation digitalization and teletransmission

Introduction

The Reason for Our Study

In August 1989 we were commissioned by you to conduct a study of 'Document Digitalization and Teletransmission.' We were to identify and analyze mechanisms:

Enabling a transition to digital storage and transmission techniques
Required for the cost-effective transmission of documents.

The 'Problems of Document Delivery for the Euronet User' were discussed in a technical report prepared by the Research Institute last year. On-line search services for scientific and technical information (STI) enable the user to identify promising references in the literature quickly and easily. But the user's needs are not met until he has a full text copy of the relevant articles, so a speedy, comprehensive and economic document delivery service is needed. The planning study prepared by the Research consultants sheds light on the requirements, problems and possible solutions for document ordering and delivery on Euronet/DIANE.

DIANE is operational today. The acronym stands for Direct Information Access Network for Europe. It represents the ensemble of information services available through the Euronet telecommunications network. Euronet itself is a data transmission facility, not an information service.

DIANE provides a framework for the services that major European hosts offer via Euronet. The hosts are typically computer service bureaus which store bibliographic data bases. By providing a medium for the introduction of common features, such as standard command language, referral service and user guidance, DIANE presents a clearer image to the user of the wide range of information services available through the network.

The EEC Committee for Information and Documentation in Science and Technology (CIDST) considered the Research Institute report, and the comments and recommendations of others who studied it, and recommended additional technical studies.

We have undertaken two of these, looking at the closely related technological, economic and managerial issues of converting documents to digital form and delivering them by teletransmission. The background to the study is the rapid development of computing and telecommunications technology that might already, or could be expected in the near future, to provide the means of electronic document delivery. This could eliminate, or cut down significantly, the movement of paper currently supplied by a document fulfillment center to a reader.

Conclusions

Our study confirmed that it is technically possible to convert a document into a digital form that can be stored in a computer data base and transmitted by digital telecommunications to printers located near to those who wish to read the documents.

The cost of digitalization and teletransmission continues to fall. However, expensive equipment is required, and large volumes of documents must be handled to achieve low unit costs. An operation planned on a European scale could deliver documents overnight at a marginal cost per page that is comparable with the charges made by fulfillment centers now meeting requests by copying and mailing documents.

We conceived a system, called DDT, which would use existing technology in a new way and looked at the organizational, managerial, legal and regulatory issues involved in establishing it as a Europe-wide operation. DDT would build on the experience gained with DIANE, and supplement it. It would be a speedy, comprehensive and economic document delivery service, accepting requests in the form of bibliographic references and fulfilling them by teletransmission from data bases of digitalized documents.

However, we believe that market forces will not bring such a system about. If the demand for quick access to full texts is to be satisfied, then a demonstration project is required.
DDT must develop as an open system, through which any information provider can deliver documents to any user. It must therefore be based on international standards.
Further technical studies are needed to determine how to apply existing technology to DDT.

1 Can we convert the printed documents to digital form?

2 Can we store them centrally?

3 Can we transmit them direct at low cost?

It would seem, then, that the analysis should have been directed at answering those three questions directly. The answers (yes, yes, and no) would then probably direct you to a deductive structure for your pyramid:

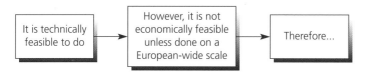

This was a situation in which the reader knew the problem, and the writer was writing simply to give a solution. Very often, however, you will write to give a solution when the reader does not know the problem, so it has to be explained in detail. That is the situation in Exhibit 35, *Period Graph Books*.

Period Graph Books

This memorandum was written for the signature of the head of the department that produces the period graph books. These are books of graphs that show company performance in sales, costs, profits, etc., for the previous period. They are made available by the staff group to managers who use them to prepare presentations to top management.

The situation within which the memorandum was written is this. The head of the department was unhappy because the graphs are full of errors. The errors are caused partly by the system used to produce them:

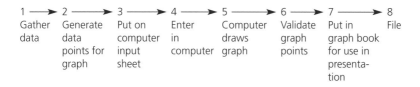

Mistakes are made in gathering and entering the data, the figures are often late or incomplete, and frequently the graph is returned by the computer too late to pick up errors in it. Even if the graphs are correct when put in the book, however, the presenter causes another problem. He may arbitrarily decide to change it to show a clearer (or more desirable) trend line. In such cases, he does not inform the staff group of the change.

The department is responsible for producing four of these books. Since the system for producing one of them utilizes the computer to gather data, the department head has reasoned that it could be used to gather data for the others.

PBG System

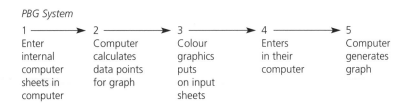

Consequently, he has decided he wants a system like this:

Proposed system

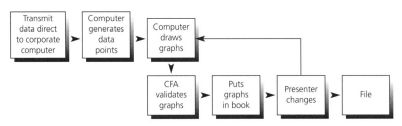

He has asked his assistant to write a memorandum to their boss, who knows about the problem, to explain the changes needed to correct it. The result is the document shown in Exhibit 35.

The document says roughly this:

S = We are now responsible for producing graph presentation books.

C = Some issues/problems have surfaced as a result of this transition.

Q =

A = This is the current production process.

This is the process for the PBG monitor book, and problems we have with it.

The problems result from the inefficient nature of the process,which needs streamlining.

At your convenience, can we discuss how best to proceed?

Exhibit 35

TO:
FROM:
SUBJECT: **Period Graph Books**

As you are aware, commencing in Period 5 the Corporate Financial Analysis Department assumed responsibility for the production phase of four graph presentation books from the Corporate Planning Department. The purpose of this memo is to outline some of the issues/problems that have surfaced as a result of this transition.

Production

In order to address these issues more clearly, I will briefly outline the production phase as it currently exists. Specific activities are as follows:

1. Data gathering – Base data sources consist of external reports (e.g. 'P' forms), internal division documents, and information relayed verbally from the division via telephone.

2. Specific data point generation – involves either manual or computerized (PBG only) calculations. For example, rolling 13 revenues, costs, and percentages (e.g., A&M as % of Net Sales).

3. Transcribe data points to input sheets – John Brennan's area supplies computer printouts of data points YTD and analysts update it for latest period's data. There is one computer page for each graph and generally each graph requires 2 new data points – actual and rolling 13. These input sheets, upon completion, are returned for updating the Colour Graphics' data base.

4. Data validation – check for reasonableness and ensure consistency of calculations.

Issues

The basic issue concerns the overall control from the point of obtaining divisional information to the actual generation of graphs. With respect to the four books transferred to the Corporate Analysis Group, this has made the control even more difficult, as it has injected one more individual into the process, and it has served to further fragment and abet an inefficient system.

In support of this, I will outline the process for the PBG monitor book and some of the related problems. The majority of PBG's monitor book calculations are computerized on a Corporate System designed solely for PBG due to the massive amount of calculations needed, since approximately 13 graphs are generated for each region.

The primary data source for input into this PBG Corporate System is the Division's internals, which are computer outputs from their systems. These results are re-input into the Corporate PBG System, which calculates rolling, YTD, per case, and percentage data points to be used for the graphs. This Corporate Computer printout is used to provide data points for Colour Graphics Input sheets. The Colour Graphics Department re-inputs these points into their data base and generates the graphs.

Exhibit 35 *continued*

As described, the process involves divisional personnel and 3 Corporate departments – Planning, Financial Analysis, and Systems. The period data in one form or another is input into a computer system no less than three times. Thus, we have created a very inefficient system and have increased the potential for error due to the number of people involved and the related fragmentation.

Some of the problems that we've encountered during the 7 periods that we've been involved are:

- Inconsistency of data input between periods and between regions.
- Incorrect calculation of Variable Costs due to the original computer program design.
- Unexplained changes in data points that were previously correct.
- Data base was not updated for prior period's information so that this Information had to be posted again on the computer input sheets.

Overall Assessment

The majority of these problems have arisen due to the cumbersome inefficient nature of the process itself. The fragmentation of the production process has resulted in no one person having control of the data and has created 'gray areas' for which responsibility is unclear. The risk of potential errors has increased, as there is the chance that things will fall between the cracks.

The production process sorely needs streamlining, both in terms of the Individual books, as well as in terms of a base computer system that would efficiently execute all of the divisions' common calculations, e.g., rolling data points. Given our current staffing, we cannot handle the production streamlining and control of the graph books.

At your convenience, can we discuss how to best proceed?

You can see that there are a number of things wrong with the document besides its poor introduction: the steps in the general system are not completely listed, the problems with the PBG system are not readily evident, and there is no mention of the changes that should be made to institute the new system.

Nevertheless, whenever you outline the problems in a system, you are by implication stating the actions that must be taken to correct the problems. Thus, as a rule of thumb you should always organize this kind of paper around the changes needed, supporting each suggested change with a discussion of the system and its weaknesses.

Visualizing the before, the after, and the differences between the two makes it easy to be specific about what the changes should be:

- Create a data link to permit transmission of data direct to the corporate computer.
- Create a reliable routine to computerize graph point generation.
- Demand that changes made by presenters be revalidated before use.

If these are the major points to be communicated, then they can form the key line of the pyramid (Exhibit 36). They serve to answer the question, 'What changes need to be made to eliminate errors?'

It is now a simple matter to work backward to determine what information has to be communicated in the introduction to induce the reader to ask that question. In this case, he need only be reminded that he knows about the problem, that he asked to have a suggested solution put in writing, and that now the document will tell him the solution.

Exhibit 36

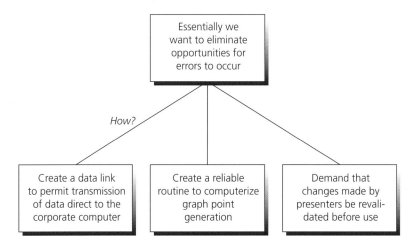

S = As you know, we have been complaining about the ineffciency of the system for producing graphs for presentations for some time

C = You asked us to look at the system and recommend the changes that need to be made

Q = (What changes need to be made?)

Essentially we want to eliminate opportunities for errors to occur

How?

| Create a data link to permit transmission of data direct to the corporate computer | Create a reliable routine to computerize graph point generation | Demand that changes made by presenters be revali-dated before use |

In most cases, with a little effort, you will find it relatively easy to visualize both the situation within which the problem occurs and the way it will look when the problem is solved. You need these to guide the writing of your introduction and to give direction to your analysis.

In doing the analysis, however, you will be creating additional structures. I'd like to look at a few of the most common of these now, to show how you can use your awareness of them to find flaws in your groupings.

Structuring the analysis of the problem

When you reach the stage of determining specifically why the problem exists, you will frequently find that the relationships you need to analyze are not directly evident. In that case your strategy should be to visualize the logical structure that must have existed to produce the results that you observe.

An excellent method for doing so is to create what are known as logic trees, of which there are several varieties. I know of five, but there are no doubt more. Let me describe these, and then go on to show how you can use the logic-tree concept to find gaps and illogicalities in what you have written.

Five typical logic trees

The great value of logic trees lies in the fact that they can often reveal where the problem is, why it exists, and what to do about it all in one picture. The trees differ slightly depending on the kind of structure being shown, but all begin at an end result and branch into causes.

1 *Financial structure.* Exhibit 37 shows an ROI tree that lays out part of the financial structure of a company, and then permits you to ask questions like 'What might cause sales to be off?' and 'What might cause that cause?' The trick is to create a mutually exclusive and collectively exhaustive group of causes at each branch.

2 *Task structure.* A deeper, more explicit approach is to make the tree show the important tasks of the business that it must organize itself to perform (Exhibit 38). To do so you begin with EPS and divide the tree in terms of the company's financial structure, stating each element as a discrete managerial task. Then you impose the Profit and Loss Account and the Balance Sheet on this structure, again stating each item as a task.

   Contribution in a cigarette company, for example, is composed of Net Sales minus Specification Costs (leaf, packing materials, duty, direct labour), minus Advertising and Promotion. These categories

Exhibit 37 Financial Structure

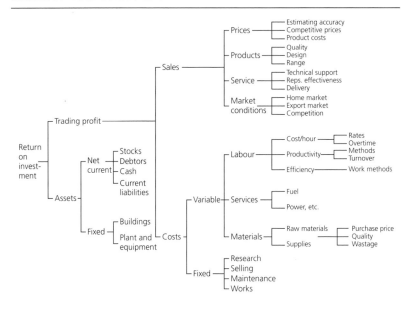

then become tasks (Increase Net Sales, Reduce Leaf Costs, etc.). You now know the key tasks of the business, and can analyze the numbers in the tree (trends, sensitivities, comparisons to industry and competition) to determine the priorities for performing them to increase EPS.

3 *Activity structure.* Yet a third approach is to use a tree to trace the activities that have to be performed to produce an undesirable end objective – high costs, for example, or overlong installation times. The trick here is to visualize all the causes that could possibly bring about the effect, and relate them at their proper levels.

For example, installation of telephone switching equipment involves work partly done in the contractor's factory and partly done by his men on the site. Elements at the site are the men doing the building, the facilities available to them, the equipment being installed, the testers testing the equipment, and the customer approving the procedure at various intervals. How do these all relate?

As you can see from Exhibit 39, you begin your tree with the effect you are trying to understand, that installations take longer than expected. At the next level you hypothesize the mutually exclusive and collective exhaustive reasons that this could occur: fewer men on each rack, more hours per man on each rack, fewer hours on duty per week. You then take each possible reason and break it down further. What could cause more

Exhibit 38 Task structure

(From *Task Analysis*, McKinsey & Company, 1972)

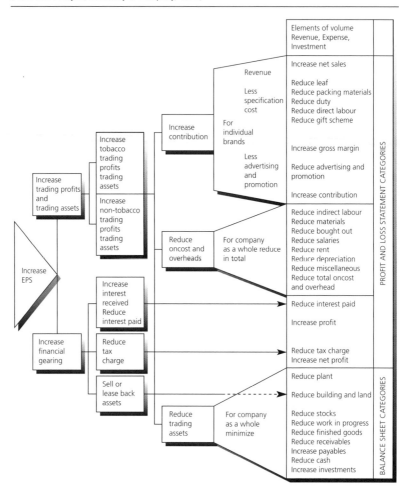

hours per man on each rack? Either the men are working more slowly, or the job demands more time, or there are unexpected delays. Again, you take each possibility and ask, why would this happen? The result is a list of the areas where facts must be gathered and analyzed.

4 *Choice structure*. This kind of tree is related to the activity structure, Exhibit 39 Activity Structure in that it attempts to find the causes of an undesirable effect. This time, however, you simply display bifurcate choices until you reach a level where you have more precise knowledge of the likely causes. In Exhibit 40, for example, if your sales support is ineffective, it can be ineffective at retail or at

Exhibit 39 Activity Structure

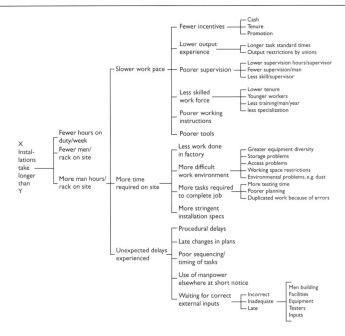

headquarters. If ineffective at retail, you can be either in the right stores or in the wrong ones; if in the wrong ones, then that is the problem. If in the right ones, then either you sell with the right frequency or the wrong frequency; if the right frequency, then either the activities are the right ones or the wrong ones, etc.

The secret to this choice diagram is to visualize the sequential process involved in selling, and reflect it in your bifurcations. First you pick the store, then you call on it, then you do the right things in it, either well or poorly. The result again is a list of the analyses that must be performed, and that will tell you how to solve the problem.

  5 *Sequential structure*. A more sophisticated version of the choice structure is what I call a sequential structure (Exhibit 41), and again I am indebted to B. Robert Holland for the example. The value of this structure lies both in its completeness and in the order in which analyses of each element are meant to be performed.

For example, your analysis might identify several indicators that your marketing programme is less than adequate. Let's say the packaging is wrong, the advertising is wrongly directed, the promotion is sloppy, and those people who do buy the product don't use it frequently enough. Weaknesses identified at the top must be corrected before those at the bottom. Thus, there is no point in trying to coax people to use the

Exhibit 40 Choice Structures

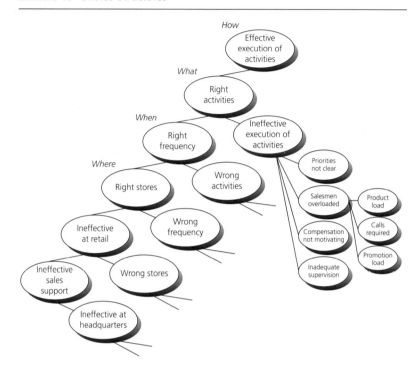

product more frequently before you get your promotional house in order, and no point in spending money on promotion if you will continue to advertise to the wrong people.

Use of the logic-tree concept

Once you understand the technique for displaying the logical relationships between groups of activities, to show their cause-effect nature, you can use the concept to question the logic of what you've written. A good example of how to do so can be seen in analyzing the *Key Issues* shown in Exhibit 42.

Here again we have a very wordy, ugly, mediocre expression of a business message. And again its impenetrability results from the lack of a clear image in the writer's mind that he wanted to communicate, itself the result of a confused approach to the problem solving.

The text was written to a company that supplies various kinds of pipes and fittings to construction sites. It purchases them from suppliers, and stocks them in a central warehouse; this warehouse in turn supplies a dozen or so smaller warehouses in regions throughout the state. The

Exhibit 41 Sequential Structure (From *Sequential Analysis;* McKinsey & Company, 1972.)

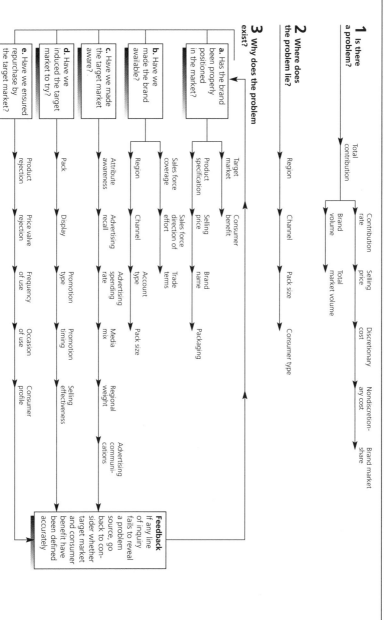

Exhibit 42

Key Issues

Based on our discussion several issues emerged that should be addressed since the answers will affect improvement opportunities, and possibly, future business strategy. These issues are preliminary only, and we would expect others to emerge.

1. Is the present inventory management system suitable for all elements of the business? We understand that a computerized 'IMPACT' type system is in use. We are familiar with systems of this type, and find them quite useful in non-manufacturing, stocking businesses in which thousands of relatively stable stock-keeping units are processed. However, it may not be as effective a method as others of determining stock levels and placing orders both centrally and in the regions.

2. With present systems, procedures, and organizational relationships, what is the level of inventory investment necessary to meet customer service objectives? A determination should be made of the investment required to serve present markets with the current products offered under existing procedures. This will provide the proper base from which to determine opportunities for improvements through change as opposed to those that could be realized through more control or discipline in the use of present systems and techniques.

3. Are centralized inventories cost effective for you? In the Piping Group, two centralized inventory pools are maintained for tube products, and valves and fittings. These pools were established when the business was small and working capital extremely limited. The central pool was intended to achieve lower inventories, lower cost, and better service, particularly for large construction projects; management is questioning this policy.

4. What are present levels of obsolete and slow-moving inventories? Excessive inventories are frequently a result of problems in this area. A key part of the analysis should concentrate on determining current inventory excesses. More importantly, we will determine the root causes so that recommendations to prevent reoccurrences can be developed.

5. With changes in inventory policies, organization structures, and systems, how much improvement can be made in inventory turn? This is the key issue, and could affect long-term business strategy. Management is willing to consider changes in long-established operating procedures if such changes can reduce the working capital intensity of the business.

company has just been taken over, and the new owners think that an inventory cost of $27 million for the central warehouse is too high. In addition, because the central warehouse is frequently out of stock of some items, the outlying warehouses also order direct from suppliers, further increasing inventory cost.

In this situation, does Exhibit 42 properly list the so-called 'key issues'? An issue, by the way, is a question so phrased as to require a yes-or-no answer. Phrasing it in this form permits you to direct your analysis to a specific end product needed to prove or disprove your understanding of the cause of a problem.

Such questions as number two, 'What level of inventory investment is necessary?' are accordingly not issues. Stated as an issue, the question would be 'Is the present level of inventory too high?' or 'Do we need as much inventory as we now have?'

Given your understanding of the problem-solving process from section one, you will be able to recognize the question as originally stated as an attempt to define how we will know when we have solved the problem. The problem now is that the cost of the inventory is $27 million, and it should be instead some other number. The first thing to establish is what that other number should be, which will prove that in fact the present levels are too high.

Assuming that the figure is too high, we can use a tree diagram to identify the possible causes of its being too high. What does one do to create inventory at high levels? Perhaps this:

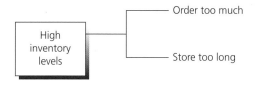

Now we can frame proper issues, which turn out to relate to points 1 and 4 in Exhibit 42:

- Is the management system placing orders properly?
- Are they holding too much obsolete and slow-moving inventory?

What does all this tell us? First, that talking about issues here is misleading. Instead, what is being discussed is the process the consultant will follow to solve the client's problem. What is that problem? That his centralized system may not be cost/effective.

He should probably be saying something like this:

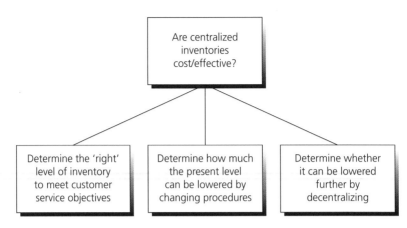

In general, I don't believe there ever is a need for a section called 'Issues' in a Letter of Proposal. The issues, if any, will always derive from

Exhibit 43 Major issues

1 How much can we reduce energy costs by improving operating practices and implementing simple, low capital engineering projects in each of the primary mills?

2 Given that we can significantly reduce energy costs by improving mill operating procedures, what is the magnitude of our cost advantage/ disadvantage compared to our competition? Is it sustainable?

3 How much of a competitive lead in lower energy costs could a sharply focused capital spending programme provide?

4 What are the right energy development programmes (i.e., research, engineering) to significantly improve our competitive position?

5 What is the best mix of fuels and sourcing arrangements to control costs and ensure supply — both short and long term?

6 Does our capital project evaluation and approval process quickly surface and implement the best energy projects to provide maximum benefits in all appropriate mills?

7 What programmes are needed to most effectively influence government funding, taxation, and regulatory action?

8 What human resources are needed to effectively manage the necessary energy tasks — i.e., organization, responsibilities, skills, resources?

9 To what extent are product/mill assignments creating a competitive penalty because of energy?

10 What is our corporate energy strategy and the business plan for pursuing it?

the analytical process to be used to solve the problem. So the issues, the process, and the end products of the study all turn out to be the same thing. (See Chapter 9 for a discussion of end products.)

'Issues' is apparently the popular buzzword in business circles these days. Exhibit 43 shows another set of issues, more confused if possible than the previous group. Here they are meant to identify the alternative ways available to reduce the cost of energy consumed in a factory.

If you tried to diagram the alternative ways to reduce the cost of energy, you would get a choice diagram like this:

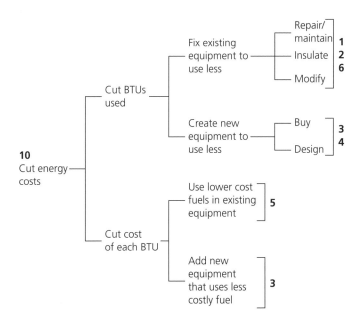

And once you have the diagram, you can see that Issues 7, 8, and 9 simply don't relate to the subject. Issues 1, 2, and 6 are related to fixing the existing equipment to use less, Issues 3 and 4 are related to creating new equipment to use less, Issue 5 speaks to using lower cost fuels in existing equipment, and adding new equipment that uses less costly fuel is touched on in Issue 3. Issue 10 refers to cutting energy costs altogether.

Remember, all groupings of ideas must have had their origin in an analytical activity of the mind. In situations where you are trying to solve a problem, the likelihood is that your groupings derived from one or another of the structures you created to guide your analysis. Matching your ideas to these structures can help you to verify their logical validity.

(The entire process of problem solving, incidentally, is called Abduction, to distinguish it from Induction or Deduction. For a detailed discussion of Abduction, particularly as it applies to scientific problem solving, see the Appendix.)

Questioning the summary statement

9

We come at last to consider the first rule of the pyramid: ideas at any level must be summaries of the ideas grouped below them, because they were in fact derived from them.

When a grouping of ideas conveys a deductive argument, the idea above is easy to derive because it is a simple summary that leans heavily on the final conclusion. But when the grouping is an *inductive* one, made up of a set of statements that you see as closely related in some way, the idea above must state what the relationship below implies.

Most writers don't state the implications of their groupings. As we have seen, their tendency is to tie together ideas that have a general rather than a specific relationship, so that nothing is directly implied. Consequently, they are forced to cap them with what I call intellectually blank assertions:

- The company should have three objectives.
- There are two problems in the organization.
- We recommend five changes.

I call these statements intellectually blank because they do not in fact summarize the essence of the ideas grouped below them. They simply state the *kind* of idea that will be discussed. As such they cannot serve as nuggets on which to focus future thinking.

This is, of course, the major purpose of summarizing a grouping – to glean an insight about which you can then think further. You will take that summary point and either find others like it (induction) or comment further on it (deduction). But you must have a true summary before the process can begin.

For example, I once worked with someone who wrote, 'The company has two organization problems' and then listed the two problems. When pressed to state how they were alike so that he could make a proper summary statement, he discovered that in fact he wasn't talking generally about 'organization problems.' He was talking specifically about 'areas of the organization where greater delegation is needed.'

Once he saw that, he realized that there were not two of these so-called problem areas, but four, only one of which he had properly identified. He further realized that his insight was that the major organization problem the company faced was its inability to delegate authority. Now having clearly stated the problem he was free to focus his thinking on finding solutions to it.

A second reason you want clear summary statements is that it makes life easier for the reader. A document studded with intellectually blank assertions is boring beyond belief to read because it does so little to anchor the reader's perceptions. In addition, there is a real danger that he could misunderstand you.

To illustrate, here is an exchange I heard on the radio several years ago:

First speaker:	John Wain says he believes he is well placed to write this biography of Samuel Johnson for three reasons:
	The same poor Staffordshire background. The same education at Oxford. The same literary preferences.
Second speaker:	I don't agree. There are no real truths in Staffordshire.

This is a superb example of the second speaker's not grasping what the first meant, because the first speaker did not in fact say what he meant. The second speaker sits poised, with his mind open, waiting for the first speaker to give him his point. But he doesn't state the point, he states 'for three reasons.'

Thus, apparently, what the second speaker heard as the major point was, 'The same poor Staffordshire background,' and his mind ignored the other two reasons. So that when he came to reply, he replied to the point he heard. The speakers were speaking directly past each other.

Now if instead the first speaker had said, 'John Wain says he is well placed to write this biography of Samuel Johnson because he and Johnson are essentially the same kind of people,' then while the second speaker would have had to listen to the three support points, he would have had to reply to the point that tied them together.

What do you have to do to make a proper summary? First, as the previous two chapters have shown, you have to check the origin of the grouping to make sure it is MECE (i.e., that its order reflects a process, a structure, or a classification). Then you look at the *kind of statement* you are making. Regardless of the origin of the idea, its expression will be either as an action statement, telling the reader to do something, or as a situation statement, telling the reader *about* something.

> • Summarize the action ideas by stating the effect of carrying out the actions.
> • Summarize the situation ideas by stating what is implied by their similarity to each other.

Thus, as Exhibit 44 illustrates, summarizing inductive groupings means either determining the effect of actions or drawing an inference from conclusions.

Stating the effect of actions

The great majority of ideas in business writing are statements of actions – i.e., statements described by such plural nouns as steps, recommendations, objectives, or changes. You use them when writing manuals, stating action plans, describing systems, or spelling out how to go about solving a problem.

Since actions are always taken to achieve some purpose, you place these ideas in a causal structure that groups them under the effect they are meant to achieve, approximately as displayed in Exhibit 45. As you can see, if you have a large number of steps to carry out in getting to the end

Exhibit 44 The Form of the Argument Dictates the Process of Summarizing

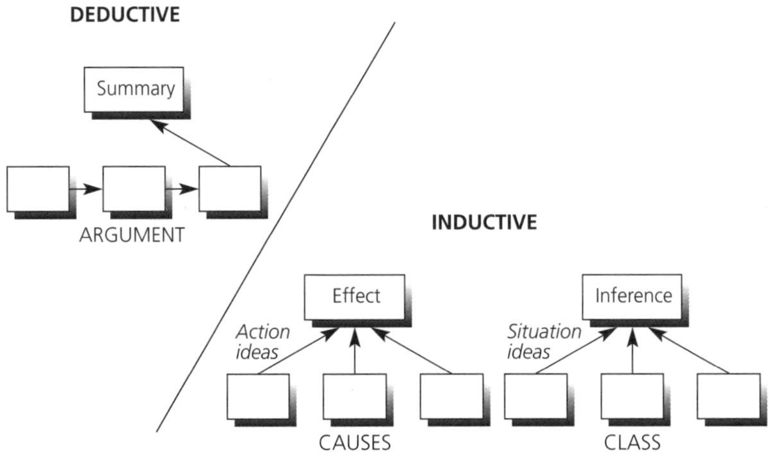

DEDUCTIVE

Summary

ARGUMENT

INDUCTIVE

Effect

Action ideas

CAUSES

Inference

Situation ideas

CLASS

Exhibit 45 Action statements should be grouped in a causal structure

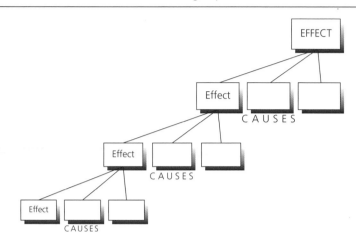

result, the hierarchical structure makes it easy for the reader to grasp how they all relate and the order in which they must be carried out.

Sorting actions by their effect is an alien kind of activity for most people, while separating various causes from various effects at a number of levels of abstraction leaves them in chaos, logically speaking. There are many reasons for this, chief among them the fact that writers habitually state actions so vaguely that it is difficult for them to determine their precise effects. In addition, very often a writer doesn't understand the difference between a cause and an effect, and in any case his tendency is to want to group by similarity, since that's his most common thinking activity. Let me suggest ways to deal with these difficulties.

Make the wording specific

If you build a causal structure properly, you will be able to say about each grouping of ideas, starting at the bottom, 'I do these three things to achieve the above effect, I do the next higher three things to achieve the next above effect,' etc. Each of the points must be mutually exclusive from the next – i.e., no overlaps – and each grouping of points must be collectively exhaustive in terms of the point at the top.

To judge whether the grouping is collectively exhaustive, the effect must be so specifically stated that it implies an end product you can hold in your hand. In other words, you can't say, 'I do these three things so that I can improve profits,' because a 10 percent improvement in profits and a 2 percent improvement in profits are both an improvement in profits, but the steps you would need to take to achieve each would differ greatly.

To be both clear to the reader and useful to yourself in checking your thinking, the point should say something like, 'I do these three things so that I can improve profits by 10 percent by January 15.' This kind of statement permits you to judge whether the steps you have grouped together underneath would in fact bring about this end result.

You will not always, of course, have a clear numerical goal as your end product. But there will always be some tangible way to judge that the step has been completed. A useful technique is to visualize a real person actually taking the action, so that you can judge how he will know when he is finished. By that criterion, this sentence is almost pure gibberish:

> A world consciousness must be developed through which every individual realizes his role as a member of the world community.

What does that mean you should do? How will you know when you have done it? Can you visualize someone 'realizing his role'? If you cannot, you do not know what the author actually means. Here is another example where you do not know:

> To reduce the chance that conflict will turn to confrontation rather than healthy debate and consideration of issues on their merits, the Task Force must be able to:
>   Handle a variety of personal attitudes.
>   Build favourable rapport with company personnel.
>   Develop good interviewing skills.
>   Plan and conduct interviews effectively.
>   Learn to gain agreement on suggestions while maintaining an objective posture.

What can the writer have had in mind? What is it actually the Task Force must do? And to what end? If they do it, what will they accomplish? As you can see, without knowing what the final objective is meant to be, you cannot judge that the steps below will in fact achieve it.

Remember that the technique is to look for an end product or cutoff point that will let you know when the step is completed. To illustrate, opposite are some examples of typically vague statements made in business writing, each translated into exactly what was meant.

You can see that each translation is easier to comprehend because it brings an image into the mind. This of course makes the document much more interesting to read. More important, perhaps, without this end-product orientation you cannot tell with confidence what the next step should be.

What was said	*What was meant*
1 Strengthen regional effectiveness.	**1** Assign planning responsibility to the regions.
2 Reduce accounts receivable	**2** Establish a system for following up overdue accounts.
3 Review management processes.	**3** Determine whether management processes need to be revised.
4 Improve financial reporting.	**4** Install a system that gives early notice of change.
5 Tackle strategic issues.	**5** Define a clear long-term strategy.
6 Redeploy manpower resources.	**6** Place people in positions of comparable responsibility.

In number one above, for example, once I visualize the planning responsibility assigned to the regions, I am stimulated to think whether anything else must be done in conjunction with this to accomplish some higher goal, if there is one. Thus, in addition to assigning responsibility, I may need to establish a planning review system to direct their activities.

By contrast, if I visualize 'strengthen regional effectiveness', what do I see? Nothing that would identify the obvious need for another step.

You will have noted that an idea can serve as both a cause and an effect in a structure. Consequently, *all* steps should be written so that they imply an end product. When your language does not obey this rule, you confuse your assessment of the proper cause-and-effect relationships. To illustrate an extreme case, take the following set of steps of what a project staff should do:

Identify high-potential profit-improvement projects
1 Review background data.
    a. Define your key task.
    b. Collect data for the key task.
    c. Review events and trends affecting the key task.

2 Identify possible projects.
    a. Measure profit impact of improved performance.
    b. Assess possible level of improvement and profit impact.
    c. Prepare a draft Profit-Improvement Project Plan.

The first step, 'Review background data,' states an essentially meaningless guideline for action. How does one know when he's finished reviewing the data? Is the end product of the review a judgment? A plan of action? Does 'review' mean read? Assess? And if you look at the substeps for guidance on the meaning of 'review,' you find that this cannot in fact be what the person is meant to do.

The purpose of the substeps (define the key task, collect the data, etc.) must be to bring about the major step stated above them. Accordingly, you must be able to ask, 'I do these three things so that what will happen?' Here the 'what' cannot logically be 'so that you can review background data.' A similar complaint can be made about the three substeps under Step 2, 'Identify possible projects.'

A good part of the writer's problem here lies in the imprecision of the language he has used to state the steps. Exhibit 46 shows, in the right-hand column, what in fact the author meant to convey by his choice of words in the left-hand column, and given that intention, what a better listing of the steps might have been.

This analysis demonstrates some common errors to look for as you group steps to form a system. Ask yourself the following questions about any grouping:

1 *Does the same step appear in more than one place?* In the original listing here, for example, the overall step and Step 2 (Identify high-potential profit improvement projects and Identify possible projects) are essentially the same point.

2 *Can I visualize someone taking the action?* If you can't, it means you have not stated the end product clearly, which makes it difficult to determine precisely what the reader needs to be told next. Try to think of the end product as being in the reader's hand at the end of the step, and then make your next statement convey an action that builds logically from this situation.

Exhibit 46

ORIGINAL STATEMENT	CLARIFICATION
1 REVIEW BACKGROUND DATA	
a. Define your key task.	a. Select an operating activity where cost and investment.
b. Collect data for the key are high.	b. Look for evidence of poor task performance.
c. Review events and trends.	c. List likely future changes in operating conditions that would make correcting performance of no value.
2 IDENTIFY POSSIBLE PROJECTS	
a. Measure profit impact of improved performance.	a. Measure profit impact of correcting poor performance.
b. Assess possible level of improvement and profit.	b. Assess the level of profit improvement actually likely to be obtained.
c. Prepare draft PIP plan.	c. Estimate the analyses required and people needed to follow up the project.
	d. Work out a timetable for their activities.

The 'Review events and trends' step, 1c on page 143, for example, is a step that disobeys this rule. The disposal to which the information about events and trends is to be put is unclear, since it does not attach logically to that gathered during the previous two steps. Visualizing someone using the end product can help you avoid this kind of vagueness.

> **3** *Will the substeps bring about the step above them?* Again referring to 1c, it is difficult to see how reviewing events and trends contributes directly either to identifying a possible project or to justifying its pursuit, the two major points in the revised listing on Exhibit 46. It probably belongs as a substep under 2a in the new listing, as something to be taken into consideration in assessing the level of profit improvement actually likely to be obtained.

Better statement of steps

HOW TO PREPARE A DRAFT PROFIT-IMPROVEMENT PLAN

1 IDENTIFY A POSSIBLE PROJECT
  a. Select an operating activity where cost and investment are high.
  b. Look for evidence of poor performance.
  c. Measure profit impact of correcting poor performance.

2 STATE THE IMPLICATIONS OF PURSUING THE PROJECT
  a. Determine the level of profit improvement actually likely to be obtained.
  b. Estimate the analyses required and people needed to follow up on the project.
  c. Work out a timetable for their activities.

---

4 *Have I kept the subject the same?* As I mentioned earlier, an action statement always implies that someone specific is taking the action. Whoever the specific someone is must stay as the same person throughout the system, or you will find yourself saying something other than what you precisely mean. Look critically at the steps given in Exhibit 47, for example.

The unstated phrase in front of each point is 'you should.' You can visualize what 'you should' do both to plan and to prepare the presentation by carrying out the steps listed below these points. But can you visualize your actions

Exhibit 47

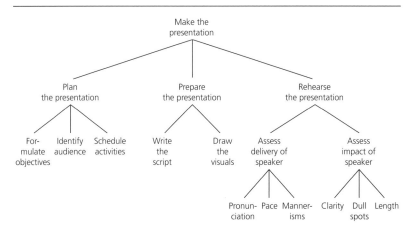

in rehearsing the presentation? Does the author mean 'you should' address the delivery of the speaker and the impact of the speaker, when in fact you are the speaker? Of course not. More likely, he means something like:

- Run through the presentation in the presence of a colleague.
- Ask him to assess your delivery and its impact.
- Incorporate his suggestions in a second run-through.

To summarize, statements about actions are sometimes so numerous that they need to be grouped. To be valid, the groupings must be arranged hierarchically as causes leading to the same effect. The wording of each cause or effect should be such as to imply a clear end product resulting from the accomplishment of the step. When it does not do so, you do not in fact say exactly what you mean. At best, that makes your writing dull; at worst, it makes it useless.

Distinguish the levels of action

Even if you get the language right, telling cause from effect can be tricky. How do you know which is which? In a causal hierarchy like Exhibit 45, an idea is an effect if you expect the reader to take the action *before* he takes the next action on the same line. It is a cause if you expect him to take it *so that* an end product can be created. This sounds more confusing than it is. For example, here is a set of steps an author is recommending that committee chairmen take before they hold committee meetings:

1. Determine the objective of the meeting.
2. Prepare the agenda.
3. Decide the items to be discussed.
4. Decide which people can contribute to the discussion.
5. Specify the end result desired of the discussion.
6. Distribute the information needed to carry out the discussion.
7. Arrange the seating.

Are these seven separate steps in a row, each one to be carried out before the next, or does carrying out some of them create others? Take the first one, determining the objective. Do I do that before I prepare the agenda, or do I do it as part of the preparation of the agenda? The only way I know how to answer that question is literally to visualize the way the agenda

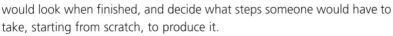

would look when finished, and decide what steps someone would have to take, starting from scratch, to produce it.

I would have thought the agenda the author is talking about contains three things:

- A statement of the objective.
- A list of the items to be discussed in order to achieve the objective, which would naturally have been drawn from the statement of the objective.
- A statement of the end result desired from the discussion of each item.

If my visualization is correct, then points 1, 3, and 5 are causes of point 2. Point 2 is on the same line with point 4, however, because it would seem that I must have the agenda in my hand, completed, before I can make a decision on which people to invite. Similarly, I must have the list of people complete before I can decide what information to send them in advance. And I would need to know what each is going to say before I can decide where is the best place for them to sit. So in fact the major points are 2, 4, 6, and 7.

That was a relatively simple example, in which it was obvious at once that you were dealing with action ideas. Sometimes, however, you will in fact be dealing with actions that you have worded as if they were conclusions.

In most cases a conclusion about the cause of a problem implies the action required to correct it. Since positive recommendations for action are more interesting to read than negative conclusions about problems, it makes sense to turn them into an action structure. For example, suppose you had drawn the following 'major conclusions':

1 Although the company's sales force has significant strengths to build upon, substantial efforts will be required near term to ensure future competitive viability.
2 Increases in sales force manpower are required to increase sales call capacity and meet intensified competition.
3 Specialized attention is necessary to improve your competitive position with chain headquarters buying offices.
4 Field representatives may not be allocating their time optimally to achieve maximum sales potential.

5 Increased merchandising requirements and the need for additional selling capacity dictate the necessity for specialized merchandising resources.

6 Significant manpower increases will require the formation of additional districts and additional management levels.

7 A formal field sales strategy is needed to provide direction to field personnel.

8 Standardized quantitative measures are needed to guide and evaluate sales resources.

The first step would be to restate those that imply actions as actions. That would mean restating all but the first one, as follows:

2 Add salesmen.

3 Assign specialized salesmen to HQ accounts.

4 Tighten account scheduling process.

5 Hire part-time merchandisers.

6 Add more districts and management levels.

7 Create sales strategy.

8 Standardize quantitative measures of work.

Clearly these are not quite in end-product terms, but that is not necessary at this stage when you are sorting out your thinking. The technique is to decide roughly what goes with what in terms of cause and effect, and then restate the points to be totally clear.

Thus, you would note that 2, 3, and 5 are all adding people, so that their effect would be to increase the size of the sales force. Numbers 4, 6, and 8 have to do with managing the sales force. Number 7 stands alone, so that roughly this is being said:

- Create a sales strategy.
- Increase the size of the sales force.
- Manage the sales force.

Why are we doing these things? Apparently to keep our competitive lead. And if we do them all, what in effect will happen? Essentially, it seems we will outcall our competition. So that you might have a structure such as that shown in Exhibit 48.

Exhibit 48

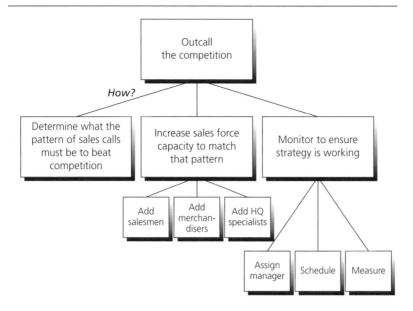

In closing this section, let me just point out that you cannot group action ideas by similarity rather than by effect. If you try to do so, you will find that you no longer have mutually exclusive groupings, nor will you be able to judge whether you have been collectively exhaustive in listing your actions.

For example, in the article on conducting committee meetings already referred to, the author said:

- The Chairman's job can be divided into two corresponding tasks:
  Dealing with the subject.
  Dealing with the people.

What this arrangement of points implies is that during the meeting the Chairman must first deal with the subject, and then when he has finished, deal with the people (whatever 'deal with' means). Obviously, you can't separate his job that way and still reflect the actual steps he has to take in the order in which he has to take them, because he sometimes has to do both kinds of things at once. The points as stated are not the effects of carrying out a coherent set of actions, and thus could not have been arrived at analytically.

Drawing an inference from conclusions What you

can group together by similarity are situation ideas – statements that can be described by such plural nouns as reasons, or problems, or conclusions. You would have classified the ideas in this manner because you believed each of them to possess a characteristic in common.

To review what you read in Chapter 7, when you say something like 'The company has three organization problems,' you have in effect taken the entire universe of possible organization problems that the company could have and made a bifurcate division of them:

You then ask yourself, 'Why these three and no others? How do I know that the division is mutually exclusive – that nothing in the right-hand oval should be included in the left?'

The only way you can know is to define the objects permitted in the left-hand oval so specifically that only the ones you have included will fit the description. In this case, perhaps 'because they are the only organization problems that result from not delegating authority properly.' What you are doing is stating precisely how these particular organization problems differ from all other organization problems in the company. You want to be as specific as possible, since the clearer your definition, the easier it is to make a general statement that applies to them all.

It is not always easy to state specifically what a particular set of ideas has in common, since it requires some creative insight. However, there is a technique you can use, which you may already have noted my using in the discussions of earlier examples. That is first to find the structural similarities in the sentences in which the points appear, and then to visualize the relationships implied between the parts that are similar.

Find the structural similarity

Ideas are always written in sentences that have a subject/predicate structure. Thus, the common property linking the ideas will usually show up because the sentences all:

- Discuss the same kind of subject.
- Express the same kind of action or object.

If the subjects are all exactly the same, you look for a similarity by which to group among the actions or objects. If the actions or objects are all exactly the same, you look for a similarity by which to group among the subjects. For example, the following statements are all complaints about the figures in an information system. They can thus be related in terms of their verbs.

1. Productivity figures for accounting, estimating, and surveying <u>should be updated</u>.
2. Regular personnel turnover figures <u>are now necessary</u> for all types of employees.
3. Competition information from tenders <u>should be gathered</u> so that the strength of competition in different markets can be monitored.
4. The present information about market rates for salaries <u>is not adequate</u>.
5. Division and project capital lockup figures <u>are needed</u>.

I will show you how to visualize these relationships in the next section. For the moment, let's look at the structure of another list. Here are the major points of a presentation given by a consultant to a client who wanted to know whether he should enter the automotive aftermarket – spark plugs, tires, etc.

1. Market is large and <u>growing</u> at an attractive rate.
2. Aftermarket is <u>profitable</u>.
3. Key market characteristics indicate high <u>barriers</u> to entry.
4. Overall trends are <u>favourable</u>, but <u>uncertainties</u> obscure some market segments' outlooks.
5. Overall, the market appears <u>attractive</u>, but is highly <u>fragmented</u>.

As you can see, since the subject is the same in each case (aftermarket), the points relate to each other by predicate. But they go together only if the predicates can be found to fall into the same category or categories. You can instantly see that there are both positive and negative points being made, so that there does appear to be some relationship. Again, I will show you how to work it out in the next section. Here I just want to show the process of matching.

Sometimes you will go through this matching exercise and *not* find any relationship at all between the points. That is always an indication that there is something wrong with your grouping and that further thinking is required before you can say precisely what you mean. Take this listing of the 'Characteristics of the Planning and Control System' being installed in a publishing company:

1 The planning cycle and its attendant control mechanism should be on an <u>annual</u> basis.
2 The plans should be built up via an <u>integrated</u> system.
3 The plans should be compiled in the context of a strong directional <u>lead from the top</u> of the division.
4 The planning system will <u>distinguish between</u> the current practice and the planned change.

These points say that the things to note about the planning system are that it is annual, integrated, begins at the top, and distinguishes between present and future. So what? That's like your telling me that your wife is five feet eight inches tall, has honey blond hair, likes green dresses, and drives a Buick. I can't put those four points together into an overall statement that will tell me anything interesting about your wife.

On the other hand, if you tell me your wife is five feet eight inches tall, has honey blond hair, wizard legs, and her measurements are 36-24-36, then I can say, 'Wow, she must be a knockout lady.' In the first case, you have made four separate comments about your wife. In the second, you have made four related comments from which I can draw a larger idea, and then continue to think about that idea.

This impetus to think further is, as I have said before, the major reason for drawing inferences in the first place. A grouping of ideas like the planning and control system characteristics above does not push your thinking upward, and therefore cannot guide it forward on this particular subject.

Visualize the relationships

How you actually draw an inference from a proper grouping is a bit difficult to explain with precision. You have assembled in your grouping a collectively exhaustive class of observations about a subject, and you now want to make a statement about the class as a whole.

Essentially the statement should give an insight into the implications of their being similar in the way they are. Achieving that insight requires a so-called inductive leap. The springboard for that leap is likely to be a visualization of the source of the relationships reflected in the grouping.

Let's look again at the first two examples in the previous section. The first group said that the information:

1 Should be updated.
2 Is now necessary.
3 Should be gathered.
4 Is not adequate.
5 Is needed.

They clearly fall into two distinct groups: those complaining that the information does not exist (2, 3, and 5), and those complaining that the information exists but is not adequate (1 and 4). So we see that the list implies that there are two problems with the information system.

Now, why these two problems and no others? What is the same about them that made the author instantly recognize them as problems that should be grouped together? Possibly because these defects indicate a uselessness for planning purposes. In that case, the point the author would state at the top would be: 'The planning system as presently set up produces information that is useless for planning purposes.' Why? Because either the information needed doesn't exist, or it exists but it's not adequate.

The next one, on the automotive aftermarket, is a bit harder. Again, the ideas fell into two groupings:

• Positive points: large, growing, attractive, profitable, favourable trends, attractive
• Negative points: barriers to entry, uncertainties, fragmented.

Clearly if the market is large, growing, and profitable, it is attractive. And favourable trends also means it's attractive. Let's visualize this attractive market with a circle, as shown in Exhibit 49.

Exhibit 49

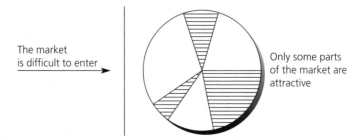

The market
is difficult to enter →

Only some parts
of the market are
attractive

The negative points don't group so easily. Fragmented means that the circle must have some segments in it, but uncertainties obscure some segments' outlooks. This means some of the segments must look different from the others. Finally, he says there are barriers to getting in, so let's show that with a line stopping entry.

Now what conclusions can we come to from the visualization?

- Only some parts of the market are attractive.
- These are going to be difficult to get into.

That sounds like the beginning of a deductive argument. The author has left off the 'therefore' point, which means he never bothered to complete his thinking. No wonder he found it difficult to write a clear summary statement of the points.

Sometimes you will be presented with groupings that look like situation ideas, but are really action ideas in disguise. Begin by treating them as if they were classed together because of their similarity, and then switch the form if you can visualize the effect that together they would achieve.

For example, suppose you read:

There are four variables to be managed in the resource allocation process:
- Sequence and timing of activities.
- Definition of specific people's tasks.
- Definition of information needs (content and form).
- Decision-making process.

Why these four variables and no others? What is the same about them that made him group them together? If you try to state them more specifically, so as to find an order, you will see that the author is probably saying this:

> The four variables are:
> - Spelling out the sequence and timing of project planning activities.
> - Specifying where decisions are needed.
> - Identifying who will participate in making them.
> - Defining the information they need to do so.

These have now become a clear series of actions. Why would I want to take these four actions? What would be the effect? I suppose it would be to fix it so that everybody who should participate does so, and does so properly. The summarizing point then might be:

> The major management task in the resource allocation process is to ensure early and substantial participation of the proper people.

Similarly, suppose you went on to say:

> Definition of content and form of information is often critical:
> - Determines what information is generated – and used.
> - Broadens perspective of participants.
> - Focuses attention on key issues.
> - Facilitates collaboration across functional and divisional lines.

Again you question. Why these four reasons and no others? What is the same about them that makes the author bring them together? You would then note that the last three have to do with the behavior of the participants, while the first one is in a way saying the same thing as the point at the top. Then why the three and no others? Perhaps he means to be saying this:

> Defining what information is needed and how it should be presented can be critical to gaining agreement and understanding:
> - Focuses the participants' attention on key issues.
> - Broadens their perspective.
> - Facilitates their collaboration across functional and divisional lines.

Before you start objecting to the difficulty of forcing your thinking upward every time, let me admit that you're not going to be enforcing this discipline absolutely rigidly throughout all your writing – not because it's not a useful thing to do, but because you don't always need that degree of precision.

How do you judge whether you've been sufficiently precise? In general, if you can think of as many points outside the group as in the group to which the overall statement could apply, you will know that it is not sufficiently precise to serve as a valid inference about the grouping. The example below from Chapter 3 falls in this category:

- Composing room costs may represent a profit-improvement opportunity:
    Low productivity.
    High overtime.
    Uncompetitive prices for simple jobs.

If I see a company that has low productivity, high overtime, and uncompetitive prices, I can infer that here is a profit-improvement opportunity. However, I can substitute three other points (e.g., high scrap yield, poor timekeeping, undisciplined systems) and still infer that there is a profit-improvement opportunity. The point at the top is too broad to make a statement about these three points and no others.

Here's another imprecise example, this time properly inductive in form:

- Japanese films are now escalating their drive for the Chinese market.
    The Toyota Motor Company sent official representatives to the Canton trade fair.
    Japan Air Lines is negotiating to fly into China.

What about Mitsubishi, or Hitachi, or half a dozen others that come to mind? Two examples do not justify a generalization about all Japanese firms. By contrast:

- The doctrinal dispute between China and Russia is still very much alive.
    Hostile rhetoric is flying between Peking and Moscow.
    Both countries are deploying troops along the border.

Here the class term is 'indications of a dispute,' and it is difficult to think of anything other than outright war that would rightfully belong in the class. Thus, the question raised in the reader's mind by the general statement will be sufficiently answered by the two points below.

The message to take away from this discussion is that you cannot simply group together a set of ideas and assume your reader will understand their significance. Every grouping implies an overall point that reflects the nature of the relationship between the ideas in the grouping. You should first define that relationship for yourself, and then state it for the reader.

Always ask yourself of any group, 'Why have I brought together these particular ideas and no others?' The answer will be either that they all fall into the same narrowly defined category, and are the only ideas that do fall into that category, in which case your summary point will be a statement about their sameness. Or that they are all the actions that must be taken together to achieve a desired effect, so that the summary point states what that effect is.

You should force yourself to justify each grouping of ideas in this way, so that you are sure that your thinking is dead clear and that your writing reflects it.

Putting it into readable words

10

You will recall I said at the very beginning of this book that writing anything clearly consists of two steps: first decide the point you want to make, then put it into words. Once you have worked out your pyramid structure and rechecked the thinking in your groupings, you know exactly the points you want to make. You also know the order in which you want to make them. All that remains is for you to put them into words.

In theory this should be a relatively easy task. One ought to be able to expect the normal business writer to translate his pyramided points into a series of concise, graceful sentences and paragraphs that clearly convey a lively message and capture the reader's interest. Alas, it does not always happen. The average sentence, far from being concise and graceful, is long-winded and heavy with jargon. This makes the paragraphs seem impenetrable and the subject endlessly boring. Let me give you a sampling:

- A primary area of potential improvement is improving cost-effectiveness of field sales-force deployment (and organization) to reflect the need for redefined selling missions at store and indirect levels dictated by changes in the trade environment.
- Preplanned adjustments may be developed from the alternative preliminary plans submitted by the Group and be in the form of outlines of contingency plans and prioritized guides to adjustments in special programmes and other discretionary expenditures.
- Current needs for accurate cash flow analyses are particularly demanding upon the existing system; it is not prepared to meet the stringent accuracy requirements. Improvements are available through incorporating information not adequately considered in making projections.

These passages were produced by bright, articulate people with excellent problem-solving skills. Any one of them can explain his ideas orally and be completely comprehensible. But they appear to believe that, in writing, the more dehydrated the style and the more technical the jargon, the more respect it will command.

This is nonsense. Good ideas ought not to be dressed up in bad prose. Works on technical subjects can at the same time be works of literary art, as the William Jameses, the Freuds, the Whiteheads, the Russells, and the Bronowskis of the world have proved. Of course technical communications addressed to specialists must employ technical language. But overloading it with jargon and employing a tortuous and cramped style is largely a matter of fashion, not of necessity.

Your objective should be to dress your ideas in a prose that will not only communicate them clearly, but also give people pleasure in the process of absorbing them. This, of course, is advice that every book on writing gives, and if it were easy to do, everyone would be doing it. It is not easy to do, but there is a technique that can help. What it primarily requires is that you consciously visualize the images you used in thinking up your ideas originally.

As must be obvious by now, you do all your conceptual thinking in images rather than in words. It is more efficient to do so. An image can take a great mass of facts and synthesize them into a single abstract configuration. Given the inability to think about more than seven or eight items at one time, it is a great convenience to be able to compress the world in this way. Without it you would always be limited to taking decisions on the basis of a few low-level facts.

But bring together instead seven or eight of these abstract concepts, and you have in front of you an enormous amount of complex detail that you can easily manipulate mentally. Look, for example, at how much more quickly you can grasp the relationships of these three lines to each other from the image than you can from the words:

A	A is longer than B
B	B is longer than C
C	Therefore, A is longer than C

To compose clear sentences, then, you must begin by 'seeing' what you are talking about. Once you have the image, you simply copy it into words. The reader, in turn, will re-create this image from your words, thereby not only grasping your thinking but also enjoying the exercise.

Let me demonstrate this process, first by showing how easily images appear when you are reading well-written prose, and then by giving you some hints on how to find the images lurking in bad prose so that you can rewrite it.

Create the image

Here is a passage from Thoreau's *Walden*. As you read it, try to keep track of what's going on in your mind.

> Near the end of March 1845 I borrowed an axe and went down to the woods by Walden Pond, nearest to where I intended to build my house, and began to cut down some tall, arrowy white pines, still in their youth, for timber. . . It was a pleasant hillside where I worked, covered with pine woods, through which I looked out on the pond, and a small open field in the woods where pines and hickories were springing up. The ice in the pond was not yet dissolved, though there were some open spaces, and it was all dark-coloured and saturated with water.

As you took in the words, did you not build up a sort of mental picture in your mind, to which you added details as you took in successive phrases and sentences? What you were building was an image, but not a photographic image. Rather it is what George Miller, to whom I am indebted for this example,* calls a 'memory image,' and it grows piecemeal as you go along.

If you read it as I did, first you see that it's March 1845, so that perhaps you have a feeling of a gray day in the past. Then you see one person borrow an axe from a second person, both indistinct, and you see him walking toward the woods, axe in hand. The trees turn into white pines, and you see Thoreau chopping at them. The next sentence introduced a hillside, so that suddenly the trees are on a hill. Then you see Thoreau stand up straight and look across at the pond, the open field, and the ice.

Your experience may or may not have been exactly like that. The point is, however, that you were *constructing the passage* as you read. The result of this constructive activity is a memory image that summarizes the information presented. You construct the image as part of the process of understanding, and the image then helps you to remember what you have read.

* From 'Images and Models, Similes and Metaphors,' in *Metaphor and Thought*. Andrew Ortony, editor. Cambridge University Press, 1979.

If you put the book down and try to remember what you read, you will probably find that you can't repeat it verbatim. But if you recall the image you can read off from it what you see, and it will be roughly equivalent to the original.

That images help to increase recall has been proven in memory studies, although these studies also show that people forget some details and embellish others, depending on their emotional predilections. Nevertheless, the memory image does provide a record of the passage and of the information extracted from it – a record that the reader constructs as he reads, phrase by phrase.

This is the kind of thing that must happen every time you read anything if you are to comprehend and remember it. Some passages are more difficult to visualize than others, and if the ideas being presented are particularly abstract, it may be that you will represent them with skeletal structures rather than with images. But unless the passage can be visualized in some form, unless the reader can actually 'see' what is being said, he cannot be considered to have understood it.

To demonstrate, here is a passage from a document that debated whether the International Bank for Reconstruction and Development should change from a fixed lending rate to a floating one.

> If the risk allowances provided in the lending rate spread turn out to be too high, the Bank's income will be returned to borrowers as a group through a reduction in the lending rate in subsequent periods. Thus, fixed rate lending would involve extra costs for borrowers as a group only if the Bank were systematically to overestimate risks and thereby earn 'excess' income more or less permanently. This possibility seems remote.

Although the concepts discussed are fairly abstract, words like 'spread,' 'excess,' and 'reduction' permit you to visualize a clear set of relationships. If asked to draw them, you could do so with no more than four lines and two arrows, perhaps like this. (I have added the words, but you would not need do so for yourself.)

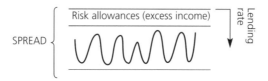

This skeletal nature of the image is important to note. One does not want a complete, detailed photographic reproduction, but only a sense of the structure of the relationships being discussed. These will generally consist of one or more geometric forms (e.g., circle, straight line, oval, rectangle), arranged in a schematized or sketchy fashion, plus something like an arrow to indicate direction and interaction.

It may seem almost childish as you look at it. But all the great 'visual thinkers' of the past who have talked about it, from Einstein on down, have emphasized this vague, hazy, abstract nature of their conscious visual imagery.

Copy the image in words

Using just these basics to create images can make a very great difference to rewriting bad prose. Let me demonstrate this using the first example on page 159. Because the words as laid out fail to call to mind an image as you read, your mind gropes in vain for something solid to hang onto. Look at the beginning of that first sentence again.

- A primary area
- of potential improvement
- is improving cost-effectiveness
- of field sales-force deployment (and organization)

By the time the field sales force arrives, the rest has disappeared from your mind. But the sentence goes on:

- to reflect the need
- for redefined selling missions
- at store and indirect levels
- dictated by changes in the trade environment.

Now, what *nouns* do we have to hang onto here that are relatively concrete? The sales force, store, and changed trade environment, perhaps. How might they be pictured in relationship to each other?

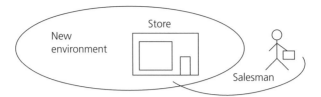

This seems to indicate that the main relationship being talked about is that of the salesman to the store. Perhaps he meant to say:

- We must redeploy the sales force to match the new trading environment.

As you can see, the trick is to find the nouns and look for the relationships between them, seeing them as a visual image. Let's apply the technique to the other two examples on page 159.

- Preplanned adjustments may be developed
  from the alternative preliminary plans
  submitted by the Group
  and be in the form of outlines
  of contingency plans and prioritized guides to adjustments
  in special programs and other discretionary expenditures.

Again, the nouns seem to be 'preplanned adjustments,' 'alternative preliminary plans,' and 'outlines of contingency plans and prioritized guides' (whatever that means). How might the author mean them to relate to each other?

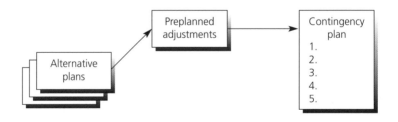

Apparently what the author wants out of the reader is some sort of contingency plan. In which case he might want to express his message like this:

> • Outline the order in which activities will be curtailed should the plan need adjusting.

One more example:

> • Current needs for accurate cash flow analyses
> are particularly demanding upon the existing system;
> it is not prepared to meet
> the stringent accuracy requirements.
> Improvements are available
> through incorporating information
> not adequately considered in making projections.

Right off, of course, we can object that it is not the system that is not prepared to meet the stringent accuracy requirements. However, to apply our process, the nouns appear to be 'inaccurate cash flow analyses,' 'system,' 'improvements' and 'information.' Might they go together in this way?

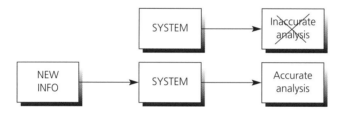

The key insight to be gained from the image is apparently that insertion of the proper information will yield accurate analyses, giving us perhaps:

> • The system can produce accurate cash flow analyses if we feed X kind of information into it.

(Without access to the author, we cannot judge what he means by 'Information not adequately considered in making projections.')

To summarize, then, a useful way to help yourself write lucid prose is to force yourself to visualize the relationships inherent in your ideas. Once you have a clear mental image, you can straightaway translate it into a clear English sentence, which your reader can just as straightforwardly interpret and absorb. And he has the additional advantage of being able to store this knowledge in his memory in image form.

Storing knowledge in image form is, of course, essential given the word-by-word process of reading and our limited ability to hold many words in our minds. By rescuing the image from the words, the reader is able not only to transfer the knowledge in large chunks, which are more efficient for his mind to process, but also to transfer it as a vivid impression, which makes it easier to recall.

To quote a kinsman of mine, Professor William Minto, who lived in a more leisured era: 'In writing you are as a commander filing out his battalion through a narrow gap that allows only one man at a time to pass; and your reader, as he receives the troops, has to re-form and reconstruct them. No matter how large or how involved the subject, it can be communicated only in that way. You see, then, what an obligation we owe to him of order and arrangement – and why, apart from felicities and curiosities of diction, the old rhetorician laid such stress upon order and arrangement as duties we owe to those who honor us with their attention.'

Go thou and do likewise.

Problem solving in structureless situations

Chapter 8 characterizes problem solving as a relentlessly logical process for discovering and displaying the underlying structures that give rise to events we consider undesirable. Our theory has been that the solution of the problem will always lie in tinkering with the structure as indeed it will if the problem is that we do not like the result the structure is yielding.

However as I mentioned, there is another kind of problem situation where the problem is not that you don't like the result but rather that you can't explain it. You can't explain it for one of three reasons:

- Because the structure does not yet exist – as when you are trying to invent something new (e.g., the telephone, underwater tunnelling)
- Because the structure is invisible – as in the brain or DNA, so that you have only the results of the structure to analyze
- Because the structure fails to explain the result – as when Aristotle's definition of force did not explain the momentum of a cannonball, or when tools rust mysteriously no matter what you do to guard against it.

It is possible that you may confront one of these structureless situations in the course of an ordinary problem-solving assignment. Although such situations require a higher level of visual thinking than we have been discussing, you will be pleased to know that the reasoning process employed is very similar.

What is required is simply another form of Abduction – a name coined by Charles Sanders Peirce in 1890 to describe the process of problem solving. In calling it Abduction he hoped to emphasize the affinity of problem-solving thinking with Deduction and Induction. Let me explain the difference between the two forms of Abduction, and show you how to use the second.

Analytical abduction

C. S. Peirce's insight was that in any reasoning process you always deal with three distinct entities:

- A Rule (a belief about the way the world is structured)
- A Case (an observed fact that exists in the world)
- A Result (an expected occurrence, given the application of the Rule in this Case).

The way in which you can consider yourself to be reasoning at any one time is determined by where you start in the process and what additional fact you know. To illustrate the differences:

Deduction

Rule:	If we put the price too high, sales will go down.	If A then B
Case:	We have put the price too high.	A
Result:	Therefore, sales will go down.	Necessarily B

Induction

Case:	We have put the price up.	A
Result:	Sales have gone down.	B
Rule:	The reason sales have gone down is probably that the price was too high.	If A then probably

Abduction

Result:	Sales have gone down.	B
Rule:	One reason sales go down is that the price is too high.	If A then B
Case:	Let me check whether in fact the price is too high.	Possibly A

We have been saying throughout that analytical problem solving consists of noticing an undesirable Result, looking for its cause in our knowledge of the structure of the situation (Rule) and testing whether we have found it (Case). You can see that this exactly matches the Abductive reasoning process shown above.

Even though Abduction is different from Induction and Deduction – and it is important to note the difference – they are also closely related. Thus, in any complex problem-solving situation you are likely to be using all three forms of reasoning in rotation. As I said earlier, the form you are using, and the results you can expect from it, depend on where you start in the process.

Where you start determines the form of thinking you will use.

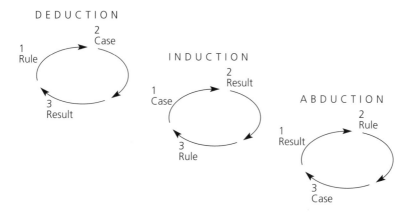

Scientific abduction

The major difference between the analytical problem solving discussed in Chapter 8 and the so-called creative or scientific problem solving discussed here is that we know the structure that creates our result and the scientist doesn't. That is, we have two of the essential elements and can reason our way to the third. He must invent the second before he can reason to the third.

In reasoning to the third, the scientist follows the classical scientific method:

- Hypothesize a structure that could explain the result.
- Devise an experiment that will confirm or exclude the hypothesis.
- Carry out the experiment to get a clear yes-or-no answer.
- Recycle the procedure, making subhypotheses or sequential hypotheses to define the possibilities that remain, and so on.

The hallmarks of the scientific method are generating hypotheses and devising experiments. Both activities demand high levels of visual thinking.

1 *Generating hypotheses*. The hypotheses are drawn out of the air, but are directly suggested by examining the structural elements of the situation that produced the problem. For example, if your problem is that you want to find a way to permit people to communicate over long distances without shouting, then you will be thinking specifically about ways to magnify the voice or amplify the ear, and your hypotheses will reflect the possibilities you envision.

Exactly *how* you go about envisioning productive possibilities is, unfortunately, not something one can spell out in a recipe. It frequently requires a kind of genius that permits you to see analogies between what you know of the problem and what you know of the world. And indeed this is what Alexander Graham Bell apparently did in inventing the telephone:

> 'It struck me that the bones of the human ear were very massive, indeed, as compared with the delicate thin membrane that operated them, and the thought occurred that if a membrane so delicate could move bones relatively so massive, why should not a thicker and stouter piece of membrane move my piece of steel.'

Clearly, we touch the tip of a very big iceberg here. No one knows what makes an apt analogy occur to one person and not to another. Certainly having total knowledge of the problem situation helps, as does spelling out and re-examining all your assumptions about it. What we do know from those who have written about the process, however, is that their insight when arrived at is always a visual image.

2 *Devising experiments*. Once the hypothesis is formulated, the next step is to use it to suggest experiments that will confirm or deny it. Again, visual thinking is required to say, 'If this structure were valid, what would follow as a matter of course? Let me set up an experiment to prove conclusively that in fact it does follow.' To put it in terms of the Abductive process:

> **Result:** I observe the unexpected fact A.
> **Rule:** A may be so because B is the case.
> **Case:** If B were the case, then C would follow as a matter of course.
> Let me check whether C does in fact follow.

We can see the process very easily in the story of Galileo and the cannonball.

Result: Aristotle says that force is that which produces velocity. From this it follows that when a force ceases to act on a body, the body should cease to move. Yet if I shoot a ball from a cannon, the ball continues to move even though the force has stopped. Aristotle must be wrong in his conception of force as it relates to motion.

Rule: I can observe the relationship between motion and force simply by dropping a ball from my hand. When I do so I notice that the situation contains three structural elements:

The weight of the ball.

The distance through which it falls.

The time through which it falls.

This suggests three different hypotheses:

Force is proportional to the weight of the body on which the force acts.

Force is proportional to the distance through which the body moves when the force acts.

Force is proportional to the time through which the force acts.

Case: If hypothesis 3 is true, then the distance covered would be proportional to the square of the time. This means that if a body covers one unit of distance in one unit of time, it must cover four units of distance in two units of time, nine units of distance in three units of time, etc. Let me roll a ball down the side of an inclined plane. This will slow up its fall sufficiently for me to measure the distances covered in different units of time, and thus determine whether the relation between distance and time is the one prescribed by my hypothesis.

New Rule: It is the same. Therefore force is that which produces change of velocity.

The trick in structuring an experiment is to make sure that it will yield a clear-cut, yes-or-no answer. It is not enough 'to see what happens' if you change one or another of the conditions in the situation. The result of the experiment must allow you to state unequivocally whether you will keep or discard the hypothesis.

It is in the sciences that have most rigorously applied this particular requirement that the greatest advances in our knowledge have occurred over the last 50 years. To quote Charles Darwin, 'How odd it is that anyone should not see that all observations must be for or against some view, if they are to be of any service.'

To bring this discussion to a close, I have set out both forms of Abduction on the next page. As you can see, they follow a common pattern. It is a pattern that can be of enormous value in guiding you to produce rapid breakthroughs in thinking about and resolving problems. Its value lies in the fact that it forces your thinking forward in a rigorous way, in the minimum sequence of steps, without dawdling or getting tied up in irrelevancies.

Each step demands a clear end product that you can literally see; each image indicates the direction in which the subsequent analyses should lead. When the problem has been solved, the images serve as anchors to guide the course of your discussion and the choice of your words.

Herb Simon says that solving a problem simply means representing it so as to make the solution transparent. I have striven to give you an understanding of the process by which such representations can most efficiently be created and utilized. We are all probably capable of thinking far more creatively and efficiently than we attempt. Clearer knowledge of the process involved might influence us to try.

Techniques of Problem Solving

Basic Process	Analytical Problem Solving	Scientific Problem Solving
1. What is the problem?	Visualize the difference between the result you get now and the result you want	Define the discrepancy between the result you get and the result you should expect to get given the prevailing theory
2. Where does it lie?	Visualize the structure elements in the present situation that could be causing the result	State the traditional assumptions of the theory that might give rise to the discrepancy
3. Why does it exist?	Analyze each element to determine whether it is doing so, and why	Hypothesize alternative structures that would eliminate the discrepancy and explain the result
4. What could we do about it?	Formulate the logical alternative changes that could produce the desired result	Devise experiments that will exclude one or more of the hypothesis
5. What should we doing about it?	Create a new structure incorporating those changes that will produce the result most satisfactorily	Reformulate the theory on the basis of the experimental results

References

1 Adler, Mortimer J. & Van Doren, Charles. *How to Read A Book*. New York: Simon and Schuster, 1972.

2 Alexander, Christopher. *Notes on the Synthesis of Form*. London: Oxford University Press, 1964.

3 Allport, Floyd H. *Theories of Perception and the Concept of Structure*. New York: John Wiley, 1955.

4 Aristotle, Logic (Organon). *In Great Books of the Western World*. Chicago: Encyclopaedia Britannica, 1952.

5 Aristotle, Rhetoric (Rhetorica). *In Great Books of the Western World*. Chicago: Encyclopaedia Britannica, 1952.

6 Arnheim, Rudolf. *Visual Thinking*. Berkeley and Los Angeles: Univ. of California Press, 1969.

7 Boole, George. *An Investigation of the Laws of Thought on Which are Founded the Mathematical Theories of Logic and Probability*. New York: Dover, 1958.

8 Bronowski, Jacob. *A Sense of the Future*. Cambridge: MIT Press, 1977.

9 Bronowski, Jacob. *The Common Sense of Science*. Cambridge: Harvard Univ. Press, 1978.

10 Brooks, Cleanth and Warren, Robert Penn. *Fundamentals of Good Writing*. New York: Harcourt Brace, 1950.

11 Brown, G. Spencer, *Laws of Forrn*. New York: Julian Press, 1972.

12 Bruner, Jerome S. and Goodnow, Jacqueline J. and Austin, George A. *A Study of Thinking*. New York: John Wiley, 1956.

13 Bruner, Jerome S. et al. *Studies in Cognitive Growth*. New York: John Wiley, 1966.

14 Butterfield, H. *The Origins of Modern Science*. New York: Free Press, 1965.

15 Cassirer, Ernst. *The Philosophy of Symbolic Forms*. New Haven: Yale University Press, 1955.

16 Chomsky, Noam. *Cartesian Linguistics: A Chapter in the History of Rationalist Thought*. New York: Harper & Row, 1966.

17 Cohen, L. J. *The Implications of Induction*. London: Methuen, 1970.

18 Cooper, Leon N. *Source and Limits of Human Intellect*. In Daedalus, Spring, 1980.

19 Copi, Irving M. *Introduction to Logic.* New York: MacMillan, 1969.

20 Dewey, J. Logic: *The Theory of Inquiry.* New York: H. Holt & Company, 1936.

21 Ellis, Willis D. *A Source Book of Gestalt Psychology.* London: Routledge & Kegan Paul, 1969.

22 Emery, F. E., editor. *Systems Thinking.* Harmondsworth, Middlesex: Penguin, 1969.

23 Febvre, Lucien and Martin, Henri-Jean. *The Coming of the Book: The Impact of Printing 1450–1800.* London: NLB, 1976.

24 Fodor, J. A. *The Language of Thought.* New York: Crowell, 1966.

25 Ghiselin, Brewster, *The Creative Process: A Symposium.* Berkeley and Los Angeles: Univ. of California Press, 1952.

26 Gordon, William J. J. *Synectics.* New York: Harper & Row, 1961.

27 Guilford, J. P. *The Nature of Human Intelligence.* New York: McGraw-Hill, 1967.

28 Hanson, N. R. *Patterns of Discovery.* Cambridge: Harvard University Press, 1958.

29 Hayakawa, S. I. *Language in Thought and Action.* New York: Harcourt Brace, 1949.

30 Hazlitt, Henry. *Thinking as a Science.* Los Angeles: Nash Publishing, 1969.

31 Holland, B. Robert. *Sequential Analysis.* McKinsey & Company, Inc. London, 1972.

32 Holton, Gerald. *Conveying Science by Visual Presentation.* In Kepes, Gyorgy. Education of Vision, Volume 1, pp. 50–77. New York: George Braziller, 1965.

33 Hovland, Carl 1., et al. *The Order of Presentation in Persuasion.* New Haven: Yale Univ. Press, 1957.

34 Johnson, Wendell. *People in Quandaries.* New Harper & Row, 1946.

35 Knight, Thomas S., Charles Peirce. New York: Twayne Publishers, 1965.

36 Koestler, Arthur. *The Act of Creation.* London: Pan Books, 1966.

37 Koestler, Arthur. *The Sleepwalkers.* Middlesex: Penguin Books, 1964.

38 Korzybski, Alfred. *Science and Sanity: An Introduction to Non-Aristotelian Systems and General Semantics.* Clinton, Conn.: Colonial Press, 1958.

39 Kuhn, Thomas. *The Structure of Scientific Revolutions.* Chicago: Univ. of Chicago Press, 1962.

40 Langer, Susanne K. *Philosophy in a New Key.* New York: Mentor Books, 1942.

41 Lerner, Daniel, editor. *Parts & Wholes: The Hayden Colloquium on Scientific Method and Concept.* New York: Free Press of Glencoe, 1963.

42 Martin, Harold C. *The Logic & Rhetoric of Exposition.* New York: Rinehart, 1959.

43 Miller, George A. *Language and Communication.* New York: McGraw-Hill, 1963.

44 Miller, George A. *The Psychology of Communication: Seven Essays.* New York: Basic Books, 1967.

45 Miller, G. A., and Johnson-Laird, P.N. *Language and Perception.* Cambridge: Harvard University Press, 1976.

46 Morris, Charles. *Signs, Language and Behavior.* New York: George Braziller, 1946.

47 Northrop, F.S.C. *The Logic of the Sciences and the Humanities.* New York: World Publishing, 1959.

48 Ogden, C. K. *Bentham's Theory of Fictions.* London: Routledge & Kegan Paul, 1932.

49 Ogden, C. K. and Richards, I.A. *The Meaning of Meaning.* New York: Harcourt Brace, 1923.

50 Ortony, Andrew, editor. *Metaphor and Thought.* Cambridge: Cambridge University Press, 1979.

51 Peirce, Charles S. *Collected Papers.* Cambridge: Belknap Press, 1978.

52 Percy, Walker. *The Message in the Bottle. How Queer Man Is, How Queer Language Is, and What One Has to Do with the Other.* New York: Farrar Straus, 1975.

53 Piaget, Jean and Inhelder, Barbel. *The Growth of Logical Thinking from Childhood to Adolescence: An Essay on the Construction of Formal Operational Structures.* London: Routledge & Kegan Paul, 1958.

54 Piaget, Jean. *Logic and Psychology.* Manchester: University Press, 1953.

55 Piaget, Jean. *The Mechanisms of Perception.* New York: Basic Books, 1969.

56 Piaget, Jean. *The Psychology of Intelligence.* London: Routledge & Kegan Paul, 1967.

57 Piaget, Jean. *Structuralism.* London: Routledge & Kegan Paul, 1971.

58 Pirsig, Robert M. *Zen and the Art of Motorcycle Maintenance.* London: Bodley Head, 1974.

59 Platt, John R. *The Step to Man.* New York: John Wiley & Sons, 1966.

60 Polya, G. *How to Solve It: A New Aspect of Mathematical Method.* Princeton: University Press, 1945.

61 Popper, Karl R. *The Logic of Scientific Discovery.* London: Hutchinson, 1972.

62 Popper, Karl R. *Objective Knowledge: An Evolutionary Approach.* Oxford: Clarendon Press, 1972.

63 Pribran, Karl H. *The Role of Analogy in Transcending Limits in the Brain Sciences, in Daedalus.* Spring 1980.

64 Quiller-Couch, Sir Arthur. *On the Art of Writing.* Cambridge: Cambridge University Press, 1916.

65 Reilly, Francis E. *Charles Peirce's Theory of Scientific Method.* New York: Fordham University Press, 1970.

66 Richards, I.A. *The Philosophy of Rhetoric.* New York: Oxford University Press, 1965.

67 Russell, B. *Logic and Knowledge.* Edited by R. C. Marsh. London: Allen Unwin, 1956.

68 Shannon, Claude E., and Weaver, Warren. *The Mathematical Theory of Communication.* Urbana: Univ. of Illinois Press, 1949.

69 Simon, Herbert A. *The Sciences of the Artificial.* Cambridge: MIT Press, 1969.

70 Skinner, B. F. *Verbal Behavior.* New York: Appleton-Century-Crofts, 1957.

71 Stebbing, L. Susan. *Thinking to Some Purpose.* London: Whitefriars Press, 1948.

72 Thomson, Robert. *The Psychology of Thinking.* Harmondsworth, Middlesex: Penguin, 1959.

73 Upton, Albert. *Design for Thinking: A First Book in Semantics.* Stanford: Stanford University Press, 1961.

74 Vygotsky, L. S. *Thought and Language.* Cambridge: MIT Press, 1962.

75 Waddington, C. H. *Tools for Thought.* London: Jonathan Cape, 1977.

76 Wertheimer, Max. *Productive Thinking.* London: Tavistock, 1961.

77 Williams, B. O. B. *Task Analysis.* McKinsey & Company, Inc. London, 1972.

78 Wittgenstein, L. *Philosophical Investigations.* New York: Macmillan, 1953.